MW01503150

Environment & Landscape

환경&조경연감 **1**

ARCHIWORLD

『발간사』

건축세계(주)는 월간 건축세계, 인테리어월드 격월간 PA(세계 건축가), IA(실내 건축가)를 발행하며 건축 · 인테리어 분야의 출판을 전문으로 하여왔다.

그 세부적인 방침으로 현대건축과 인테리어를 집중 소개, 분석하여 건축 · 인테리어 디자인의 정체성을 확립하려는 노력을 경주하여 왔으며 건축 · 인테리어 전문분야의 선도적 언론문화를 창달하고자 최선을 다하고 있다.

아울러 인간, 환경, 공간에 대한 관심과 중요성이 높아지고 있는 현 상황에 환경디자인 자료에 대한 부분의 부족함을 통감하여 본지는 금년부터〈환경과 조경 연감〉을 발간하게 되었다.

최근 환경조경과 디자인의 모범사례가 될 완공작을 선별하여 취재 · 편집하였으며 아파트단지와 빌딩을 중심으로 아파트편, 건물편, 공원 & 기타로 구분하였다.

이는 21세기 환경시대를 맞이하여 국내 · 외의 환경디자인 흐름을 파악할 수 있는 초석이 될 것이며, 공식적으로는 충실한 자료집이 될 수 있으리라 믿는다. 모쪼록〈환경과 조경 연감〉을 통하여 당대 환경디자인의 알찬 정보와 혜안을 얻길 바란다.

끝으로〈환경과 조경 연감〉책자를 엮는데 자료협조 및 사진촬영에 협조해 주신 조경 · 건축 · 조각가 및 건축주께도 깊은 감사의 말씀을 드린다.

특히 본지를 사랑해 주시는 독자 여러분에 대한 기대에 부응하기 위해 앞으로도 알찬 내용과 편집으로 만나 뵐 것을 약속드리며 지속적인 관심과 편달 부탁드린다.

2004년 2월
발행인 정 광 영

「Address for Publication」

Archiworld Co., Ltd. publishes Monthly Archiworld, Interior World, Bimonthly PA(Pro Architect) and IA(Interior Architect). We have made our best to establish identity and create a leading journalism culture in the field of architecture and interior design. Today as three factors-space, human, and environment-attract great attention, we publish 〈Environment and Landscape Annual〉 series to meet needs for it.

It contains carefully selected completed works which would be good examples of recent environment landscape and design. The book involves sections of Apartments, Buildings, Park & others, centering on apartments and buildings.

These books, full of great materials, will lay a cornerstone of understanding the trend of domestic environment design for the 21st environmental period to come. It's my pleasure for you to get information and keen insight about the current environment design through these books.

In conclusion, I'd like to express my heartfelt thanks to many architects, landscape architects, sculptors, and owners for providing good materials and helping us take photographs. Also, I will do my best to at up to readers' expectation with good contents. I would appreciate your continuous attention and advice.

Thank you.

Feb. 2004
Publisher Jeong, Kwang Young

Contents

Apartment / 아파트

Universiade Athletes' Village, Daegu
대구 유니버시아드 선수촌 아파트　　8

Samsung Raemian, Seocho-dong
서초동 삼성래미안　　16

Lotte Spa Castle, Seocho-dong
서초동 롯데 스파 캐슬　　24

Samsung Raemian, Dogok-dong
도곡동 삼성래미안　　32

Lotte Nakcheondae Apartment, Ujangsan
우장산 롯데 낙천대 아파트　　40

Hyundai Home Town, Munllae-dong
문래동 현대 홈타운　　50

Daelim Village in Bojung, Yongin
용인 보정 대림 빌리지　　58

Lotte Castle Galaxy, Jamwon-dong
잠원동 롯데캐슬 갤럭시　　68

I-Space, Bundang
분당 아이 스페이스　　76

Tower Palace, Dogok-dong
도곡동 타워팰리스　　88

Seohai Grand Bleu in Sang-dong, Bucheon (8, 12BL)
부천 상동 서해 그랑블(8, 12블럭)　　94

Samsung Apartment in Munhyeon-dong, Busan
부산 문현동 삼성아파트　　104

Lotte Castle Park, Bangbae-dong
방배동 롯데 캐슬 파크　　114

Samsung 5-cha Apartment, Suji
삼성 수지 5차 아파트　　122

Seocho Garden Suite
서초 가든 스위트　　128

LG Metro City in Yongho-dong, Busan
부산 용호동 LG 메트로시티　　134

Daelim (World Town) e-Pyeonhan Sesang, Sungsan
성산 (월드타운) 대림 e-편한세상　　138

Chuncheon Dumir Military Apartment
춘천 두미르 군인아파트   148

Daelim e-Pyeonhan Sesang, Daebang-dong
대방동 대림 e-편한세상   154

Daelim e-Pyeonhan Sesang 5, 6-cha, Sindorim
신도림 5, 6차 대림 e-편한세상   164

Building / 건물

Jeju International Convention Center
제주국제컨벤션센터   172

Kyobo Tower
교보타워   186

Geoje Culture Arts Center
거제문화예술회관   200

Kitakyushu Environment Museum
기타큐수 환경박물관   210

Tseung Kwan O Community Center, Hong Kong
홍콩 Tseung Kwan O 커뮤니티센터   218

Mayfield Hotel
메이필드 호텔   228

Hong Kong University of Science & Technology
홍콩 과학기술대학교   236

Park & others / 공원 & 기타

Namgaram Culture Street in Manggyeong District, Jinju
진주시 망경지구 남가람 문화거리   246

Sculpture & Light for Ayang Bridge
아양교 조형물 및 경관조명   254

Daegu Duryu Park
대구 두류공원   266

Yeolin Madang - Plaza in front of Dong-gu Office, Daegu
대구 동구청앞 광장 - 열린마당   278

Suwon World Cup Stadium
수원 월드컵 경기장   286

Environment & Landscape
환경 & 조경 연감 ①

Publisher   Jeong, Kwang-young
발행인   정광영

Reporter   Ko, Moon-sun
취재기자   과장 고문순
                     Hong, In-ju
                     대리 홍인주
                     Yoo, So-hwi
                     대리 유소휘
                     Jang, Yun-sun
                     장윤선
                     Jun, Hyun-young
                     전현영

Designer   Jeon, Mi-sook
편집디자인   과장 전미숙
                     Jin, Kyung-ju
                     진경주

Photograph   Kim, Myoung-sik
사진   김명식
                     Kwon, Yong-koo
                     권용구
                     Kim, Kyung-youn
                     김경연

Executive director   Ko, Se-hwan
이사   고세환

Managing   Jeong, Sun-yeong
전무   정선영

Publishing : ARCHIWORLD Co., Ltd.
발행처 : 건축세계(주)
Mailing Add : 222-11 Bangi-dong Songpa-gu
             Seoul, Korea
주소 : 서울시 송파구 방이동 222-11 건축세계빌딩
TEL : 82-2-422-7392   FAX : 82-2-422-7396

발행일 : 2004년 2월 7일
Single Copy : US $68
정가 : 68,000원
분해출력 : (주)삼진프린테크
인쇄 : 조일문화인쇄소

구입 및 광고문의
전화 : 02-422-7392(총무부)
팩스 : 02-422-7396,9
e-mail : aid@archiworld-pa.com
http ://www.archiworld-pa.com

ⓒ 건축세계(주)
Printed in Korea

Apartment

Universiade Athletes' Village, Daegu

Samsung Raemian, Seocho-dong

Lotte Spa Castle, Seocho-dong

Samsung Raemian, Dogok-dong

Lotte Nakcheondae Apartment, Ujangsan

Hyundai Home Town, Mullae-dong

Daelim Village in Bojung, Yongin

Lotte Castle Galaxy, Jamwon-dong

I-Space, Bundang

Tower Palace, Dogok-dong

Seohai Grand Bleu in Sang-dong, Bucheon (8, 12BL)

Samsung Apartment in Munhyeon-dong, Busan

Lotte Castle Park, Bangbae-dong

Samsung 5-cha Apartment, Suji

Seocho Garden Suite

LG Metro City in Yongho-dong, Busan

Daelim (World Town) e-Pyeonhan Sesang, Sungsan

Chuncheon Dumir Military Apartment

Daelim e-Pyeonhan Sesang, Daebang-dong

Daelim e-Pyeonhan Sesang 5, 6-cha, Sindorim

▲ The stroke – Baik, Chul soo

건축설계 : (주)DST종합건축 + (주)토담건축
조경설계 : 기술사무소 동인조경마당 (02)2202-0293
조경시공 : 현대건설, 화성산업
위　　치 : 대구시 북구 동서변 택지개발사업지구 내
대지면적 : 1단지 – 46,545㎡, 2단지 – 53,830㎡
연 면 적 : 1단지 – 122,475.8789㎡,
　　　　　　2단지 – 138,679.6656㎡
건축면적 : 1단지 – 8,760.8994㎡
　　　　　　2단지 – 10,148.7826㎡
녹지면적 : 1단지 – 14,430.32㎡, 2단지 – 14,547.23㎡
건 폐 율 : 1단지 – 18.82%, 2단지 – 18.85%
용 적 률 : 1단지 – 202.10%, 2단지 – 199.85%
세 대 수 : 1단지 – 780세대, 2단지 – 1,160세대

Architect Design : Dong Sing Tech Architects &
　　　　　　　　　　Associates Inc. +
　　　　　　　　　　TODAM Architects & Engineers
Landscape Design : Landscape Architects &
　　　　　　　　　　Associates MA DANG
Landscape Construction : Hyundai Engineering &
　　　　　　　　　　Construction + Hwasung
　　　　　　　　　　Industrial Co., Ltd.
Site Area : 1BL – 46,545㎡, 2BL – 53,830㎡
Total Area : 1BL – 122,475.8789㎡,
　　　　　　　2BL – 138,679.6656㎡
Built Area : 1BL – 8,760.8994㎡
　　　　　　　2BL – 10,148.7826㎡
Green Area : 1BL – 14,430.32㎡
　　　　　　　2BL – 14,547.23㎡
Building Coverage Ratio : 1BL – 18.82%,
　　　　　　　　　　　　　2BL – 18.85%
Floor Area Ratio : 1BL – 202.10%, 2BL – 199.85%
Household : 1BL – 780 Families
　　　　　　　2BL – 1,160 Families

▲Bird's eye view

▲Sky sloping — Lee, Young song (1BL)

이곳은 '대구 유니버시아드 선수촌'으로 활용하기 위한 목적으로 건립된 아파트 단지로 세계 젊은이들의 축제의 장으로서 의미와 축제에 부합된 단지환경 조성은 물론 추후 입주하는 주민들에게는 편안한 삶의 터전이 되어야 하는 양면성이 계획 초기부터 고려되었다.

축제의거리는 기존 주공단지와 새로이 조성되는 1단지와 2단지를 연결하는 가로로 보다 차별화된 지역커뮤니티의 중심도로 및 활성화된 가로가 되도록 고려되었다.

'열린마음 열린마을'과 '야외갤러리가 있는 푸른마을'이라는 부제를 가진 본 프로젝트는 팔공산자락인 학봉에서 단지외곽을 두르듯 흐르는 동화천과 금호강으로 연결되는 오픈스페이스로 계획되었다.

또한 조각심포지엄을 통해 여러 작가들이 한데 모여 작품을 제작함으로써 유니버시아드 대회의 축제분위기를 고양하고, 실제 생활공간 속에서 예술적 가치를 부여하였다.

This condominium complex has been built for the athletes' village of Daegu Universiade. From the early stage of this project, therefore, we set up the plan not only to create an environment that could meet the meaning of youths' festival place and the festival itself but also to make a convenient living place for those who would move in this condominium complex to live in the future.

For the road that would link the existing Joogong complex to the newly built 1st complex and 2nd complex of this condominium, we considered it more activated road as the central road of this local community that would be more differentiated.

In this project that we carried out with the subtitles, 'Open Mind, Open Village' and 'Green Village in which there is an Open Gallery', we planned to make an open face that would go from Hakbong, a part of Palgong Mt., through to Donghwa stream and Keumho river.

For this project, besides, many architects gathered to work in order to raise up the festival mood of Universiade Game and grant artistic value to this actual living space.

▲No title – Kim, Young won (1BL) ▼Metaphor – Shim, Moon seup (1BL)

▲Central plaza (1BL)

▲Central plaza (2BL)

1BL

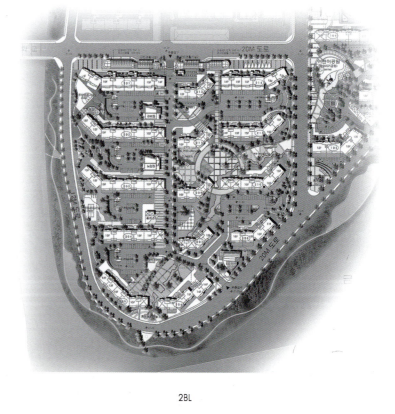

2BL

Master plan

▲Wings – Philippe Desloubieres

▲Dice – Gabrielle Wambaugh (1BL)

▲Hole in Space Time – Hiroyuki Asano (1BL) ▼No title – Hyun, Hye sung (1BL)

▲Tension − Caterina Tarantino

▲Judgment − Oh, Sang il

▲Man−Nature − Lee, Jong bin

Samsung Raemian, Seocho-dong

조 경 설 계 : 김종해조경설계(주) (031)704-8051~2
시　　　공 : 삼성물산 건설부문
조 경 시 설 : 청우개발
조 경 식 재 : (주)고운조경
위　　　치 : 서울시 서초구 서초동 1682번지
대 지 면 적 : 45,939㎡
조 경 면 적 : 15,268㎡
세 대 수 : 1,129세대

Landscape Design : Kim Jong Hae Landscape design
Construction : Samsung Engineering & Construction
Landscape Facilities : Chung Woo Development
　　　　　　　　　　　　　Corporation
Landscape Planting : Gown Landscape architacture
Site Area : 45,939㎡
Landscape Area : 15,268㎡
Household : 1,129 Families

▲Central plaza

▲Landscape arts

'단지속의 공원' 이라는 말이 가능한 곳이 '서초 삼성 래미안' 이다. 단지 중앙에 대단위 녹지를 설계해 그 주위로 소나무 군락을 이룬 중앙공원은 전체적으로 정갈하고 고즈넉한 분위기를 자아낸다.

1층 필로티 사이로의 원활한 동선을 이루는 이 공간은 소나무 숲 사이로의 휴게공간이 형성되었으며 노인정, 유치원, 운동시설 등 중앙공원의 주변으로 형성되어 단지 안에서도 녹음의 아름다운 공원을 볼 수 있도록 설계되었다.

지형의 고저차에 의해 만들어진 어린이 놀이터는 섬 형태의 모습으로 흥미감을 일으키며 주변으로의 다단식 녹지대 형성은 경사에 대한 위험을 덜어준다. 이런 모든 공간들은 중앙 공원으로부터 동선이 연결되어 작은 산책로처럼 이어진다.

이 공간은 한 장소의 특화된 장소를 만들자는 의도가 아닌 삭막해져가는 아파트 단지 안에 하나의 작은 따스함이 느껴지는 초록의 공원을 만들고 싶은 생각에서 설계되었으며, 편안하게 쉴 수 있는 자연을 보여주고자 노력하였다.

It is 'Samsung Ramian in Seocho-dong' that can be called 'a park in a condominium complex'. Very spacious green field were designed to be located at the center of this complex to form the central part, around which pine community were made, so that it could make a well-organized and calm circumstance. In this space that makes a smooth moving-line between the 1-story pilotis, several resting spaces have been formed in the pinewoods. Several facilities including an old people's community center, kindergarten, athletic facilities and etc were designed to be around this center park, so that the beautiful green park could be seen even in the condominium complex. The children's playground that is made based on the ground altitude difference looks an island attracting the interests of people. The slope of this playground that may be dangerous could be safer by forming the multi-story green field around this area. All these spaces are connected with the central park through the moving-lines, which are all connected as a small walkway.

The central park space was designed based on the idea not to make a special space but to make a green park in which the residents could feel warm in a condominium complex that could make people dry. This park was designed to also show the nature in which people could relax.

▲Pathway

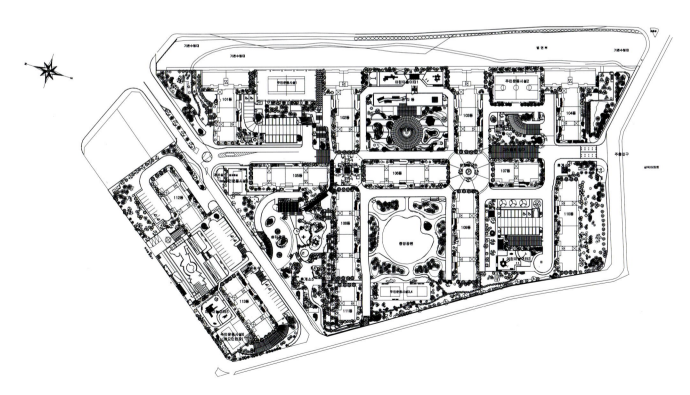

Master plan

▲Central park

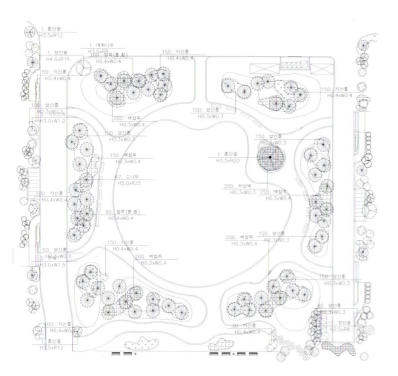

Part plan

▲Sketch

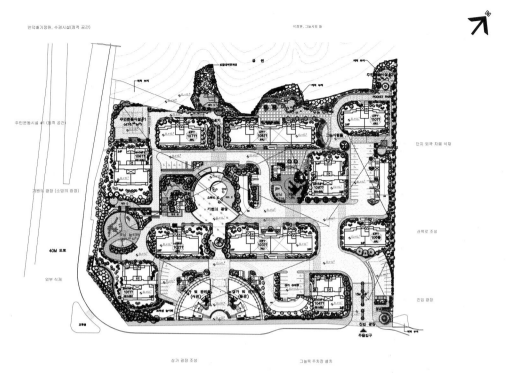

Master plan

매봉산과 40m 도로의 남부순환로와 선릉로 등이 교차하는 대로변에 위치한 본 부지의 특성을 살려 매봉산의 자연을 차경요소로 도입하고, '도곡동' 이라는 지명 유래에서 '돌' 이라는 요소를 찾아 설계 모티브로 설정하며 문주, 담장, 장식벽 등의 시설물과 포장계획에 활용한다.

단지의 남북의 중심보행축(종축)은 소나무 군식으로 비스타을 형성하며 단지 차량축(횡축)은 선주목길, 향나무길로 상로수길을 조성하고 진입광장, 그늘시렁뜰, 주민운동시설에는 팽나무, 은행나무, 청단풍 등의 초점목을 식재한다.

- 기원의 광장 : 구조체를 지양한 큰 규모의 오픈 스페이스 광장으로 잔디광장과, 괴석(소망의 돌)조형물, 화강석 앉음벽 등의 시설물 계획과 해와 달의 자전축을 마천석 물갈기로 표현하여 해넘이선을 조성한다.

- 언덕배기정원 · 석정원 : 매봉산자락과 만나는 전이공간으로 마른폭포와 건천을 도입하고 기존 수림대와의 조화로운 식재군을 형성하여 기존수림대(참나무림)를 보존하고 유지하는 경관으로 조성한다.

- 계곡정원 : 정적이고 반개폐적인 공간으로 해미석 박기와, 답석포장으로 오솔길을 걸어가는 정다운 분위기를 유도하며 부지내 2m 단차를 극복하기 위한 방안으로 현대적이고 세련된 장식벽을 설치해 위요감을 조성한다.

그 밖에 주진입광장은 천연석문주, 장식벽, 성곽석 쌓기 등으로 단지의 상징성을 높이며, 단지 중심축의 초입광장인 상가광장은 경관의 프레임 역할을 위한 트렐리스 게이트를 설치한다. 가로공원과 필로티 공간, 순환 산책로를 조성하여 인근 주민에게 편익을 제공하고 또 하나의 휴게광장으로 이용 될 수 있도록 하여 공간의 활용성을 높인다.

The site is located where Maebongsan, 40m South Belt Way and Seonrengro are crossing. Utilizing its location, the architect adopted the nature of the Maebongsan as the secondary landscape factor and made 'stone' a design motive after the name of the site 'Dogok-dong', using it on facilities like a gatepost, wall, decoration wall and pavement plan. The central south-north walking road (vertical axis) forms a vista with pines and car streets (horizontal axis) are set with pines, aromatic trees, and evergreens. The entry square, shade garden, and outdoor exercise facilities for residents have nettle trees, ginkgo trees, and blue maples planted as focus trees.

- Prayer Square : This is a large open space as an upgraded structure. It consists of a lawn square, facilities plans such as grotesque stone sculpture (Stone of Hope), granite sitting wall and sunset line, by representing the rotating axis of the sun and the moon as a polished marble stone.

- Garden on the slope/stone garden : A transition site that meets the skirt of Maebongsan. A dry wall and dry stream have been established and the garden forms a tree community harmonizing with existing ones. This site preserves and maintains the original forest (aromatic trees) as a landscape.

- Valley garden : A stagnant and semi-opened space with gravel and stepping stone pavement, which yields a warm atmosphere as a walk path. Also, modern and elegant art wall was introduced to overcome 2m of floor gap in the complex, creating separation feeling.

For others, the main entry square emphasized the symbol of the complex with natural-stone-made gatepost, decoration wall, stonewall built in. Mall square that the initial entry square of the central axis was furnished with trellis gate working as a frame of the landscape. Roadside park, piloti site, walk path provide residents with convenience and widen the area's application by making that function as a rest area.

▲Promenade

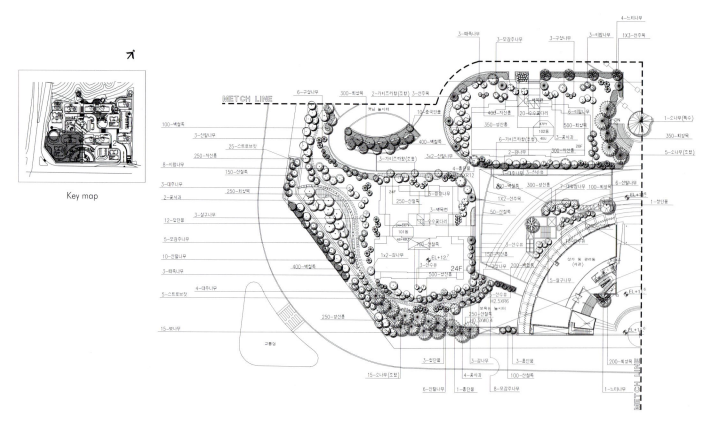

Key map

Planting plan-1

▲Deck

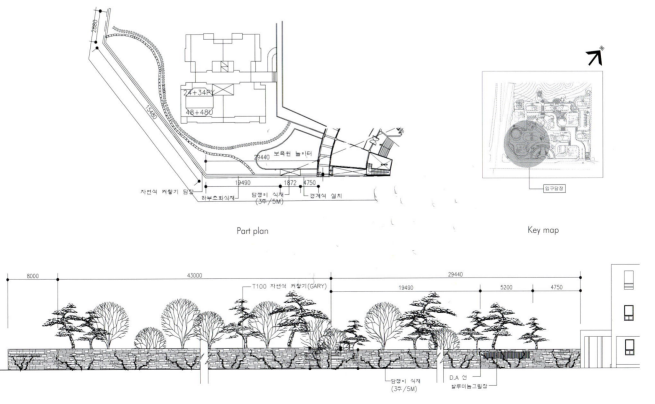

Part plan

Key map

Elevation

▲Playground

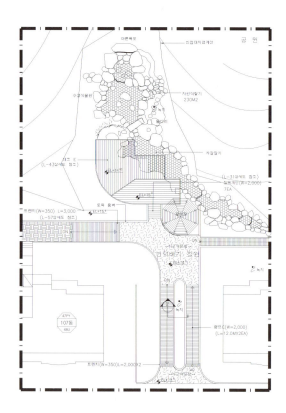

Part plan

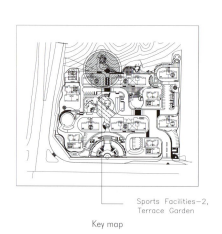

Sports Facilities-2,
Terrace Garden

Key map

Ramp "C" section

▲Entrance

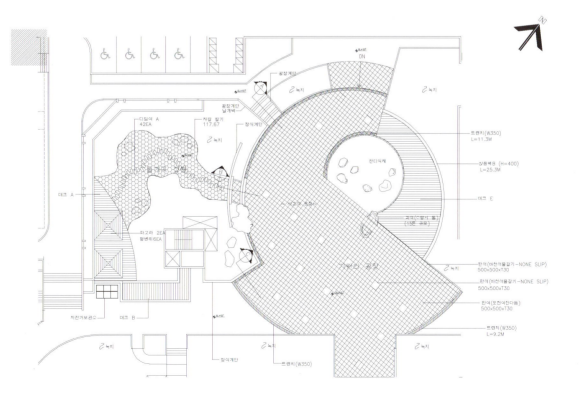

Central plaza

▲▼Pergola

Lotte Nakcheondae Apartment, Ujangsan

조경설계 : (주)성호엔지니어링 (02)566-9996
건축설계 : (주)나우동인건축사사무소
시   공 : 롯데건설(주)
위   치 : 서울시 강서구 화곡동 1145번지
대지면적 : 66,508.50㎡
건축면적 : 11,994.07㎡
연 면 적 : 235,741.47㎡
조경면적 : 22,319.87㎡
녹지면적 : 10,029.63㎡
건 폐 율 : 18.03%
용 적 률 : 256.86%

Landscape Design : Sungho Engineering Co., Ltd.
Architecture Design : NOW Architects
Construction : LOTTE Engineering & Construction
Site Area : 66,508.50㎡
Built Area : 11,994.07㎡
Total Floor Area : 235,741.47㎡
Landscape Area : 22,319.87㎡
Green Area : 10,029.63㎡
Building Coverage Ratio : 18.03%
Floor Area Ratio : 256.86%

▲Symbolic sculpture & Curtain fountain

▲Wooddeck Resting place

이곳 우장산 롯데 낙천대 아파트는 우장근린공원을 끼고 자리잡아 다른 곳보다 뛰어난 조망을 자랑한다. 다른 아파트 부지보다 기본적으로 녹지면적이 주변으로 많이 이루어져 있어 쾌적한 환경조성은 물론이고 각각의 동마다 잘 정돈되어있는 조경 시설물들은 그 동선과 배치에 있어 편리한 생활환경을 조성해준다.

가운데의 낙천대 광장을 중심으로 단지마다 휴게공간과 놀이공간이 멀지 않게 잘 배치되어있으며 그 이외에 주민운동시설공간과 어귀마당, 롤러스케이트장의 위락 공간들이 자리 잡아 사람들의 커뮤니케이션이 오갈 수 있는 삶의 활력을 불어넣어주는 장으로 이용될 것이다. 입구마당의 커튼분수를 중심으로 꾸며진 여러 공간들이 아파트라는 약간의 삭막한 공간을 따뜻하고 활력이 넘치는 장으로 만들어 주기를 기대한다.

This Lotte Nakchundae Condominium is located in the neighborhood of Woojang mountain Park, so this has greater view than the others have. This condominium complex forms pleasant environment because it basically has more green field area around itself than the other condominium complexes' area. Besides, the landscape facilities that are well organized for each building forms a convenient living environment in the aspect of their moving line and disposition.

The space for taking rest and playground are disposed not far from each other at every complex with Nakchundae plaza centered. Besides, the recreational spaces such as residents' athletic facility, arbor ground and in-line skate ground will be also playing the role of instilling the life energy in the residents so that they can communicate to each other. Various spaces decorated with the curtain fountain centered are expected to help this condominium that can be a little bit dreary space becoming a place that is warm and full of energy.

▲Landscape arts

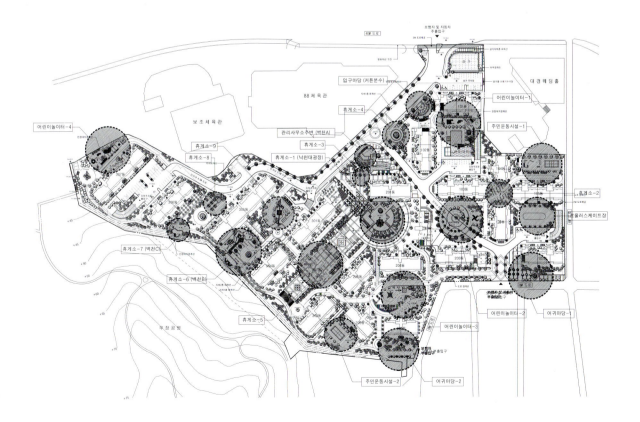

Master plan

■ Wall fountain

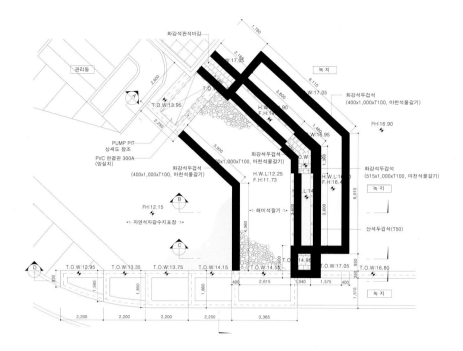

Part plan

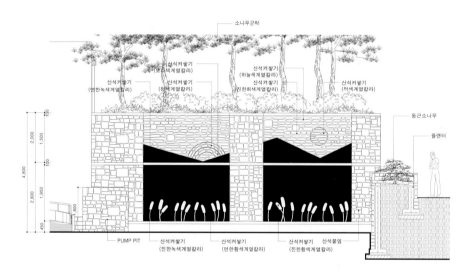

Elevation & Section - A

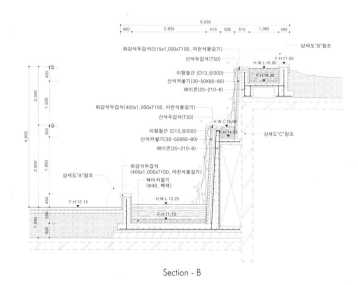

Section - B

Section - C

▲Pavilion

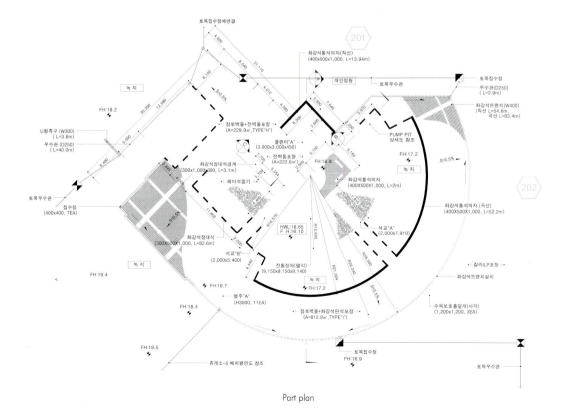

Part plan

▲Pavilion

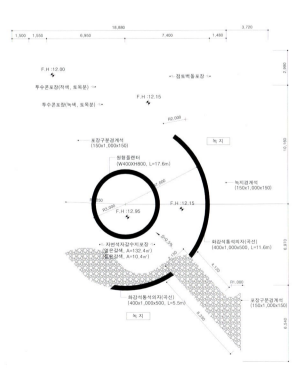

Part plan

▲Resting place▼Pathway

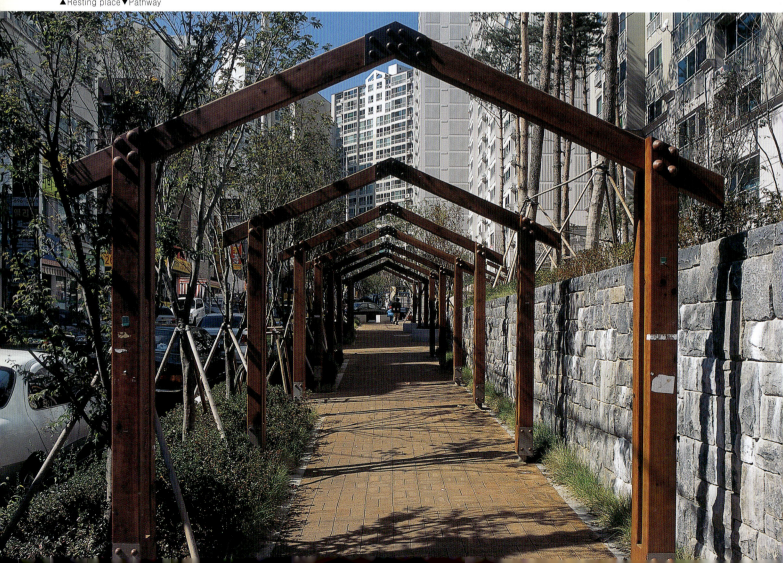

▲Curtain fountain

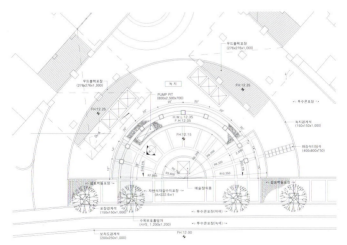

Part plan

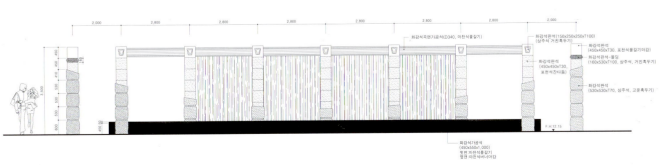

Elevation

Hyundai Home Town, Mullae-dong

조경설계 : (주)그룹 · 한
위   치 : 서울특별시 영등포구 문래동 3가
           77-19 외 8필지
대지면적 : 68,748.80㎡
조경면적 : 25,523.98㎡ (대지면적의 37.12%)
준 공 일 : 2003. 6

Landscape Design : Group · Han Co., Ltd.
Site Area : 68,748.80㎡
Landscape Area : 25,523.98㎡ (37.12% of site area)
Completion : 2003. 6

▲Bird's eye view

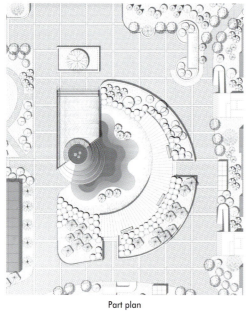

Part plan

▲Promenade & Resting place

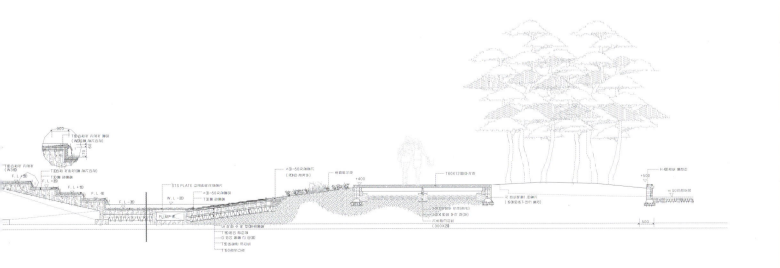

Elevation

▲Pathway ▼Playground

▲Playground(Sik−Holz)

▲Pathway ▼Playground

▲Pathway

Master plan

▲▼Resting place

▲Master plan

▲Bird's-eye view

▲Entrance colonade

조 경 설 계 : 지·오조경기술사 사무소 (02)501-0935
건 축 설 계 : (주)기단종합건축사사무소
시   공 : 대림산업(주)
조 경 식 재 : 영원산업개발(주)
조경시설물 : 청우개발
위   치 : 용인시 구성읍 보정리
대 지 면 적 : 49,708㎡
연 면 적 : 50,562㎡
조 경 면 적 : 22,184㎡
용 적 률 : 87.21%

Landscape Design : G·O Landscape Architecture &
                                 Associates
Architecture Design : Gidan Architects & Engineers
Construction : Daelim Industrial Co., Ltd.
Landscape Planting : Youngwon Industry
                                 Development Corporation
Landscape Facilities : Chung Woo Development
                                 Corporation
Site Area : 49,708㎡
Total Floor Area : 50,562㎡
Landscape Area : 22,184㎡
Floor Area Ratio : 87.21%

▲ garden

▲Pathway▼Playground

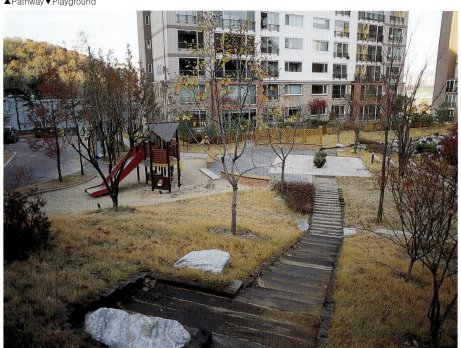

용인보정 대림 빌리지는 부지를 감싸안듯 둘러진 푸른 숲과 산기슭 사이로 여유롭게 흘러내리는 맑은 계류, 고속도로를 사이로 펼쳐진 녹색들판, 살랑이는 바람결을 허허롭게 맞을 수 있는 전형적 도시근교의 전원형 택지이다.

전체 지형은 10% 내외의 경사지로써 일부 포장면을 제외하면 넓은 평탄 가용지는 그리 많지 않다. 따라서 화계를 통해 지형과 순응하며 두 개의 계류를 단지 내로 흘리고, 모아서 솟구치고, 떨어뜨릴 수 있는 수(水)공간을 조성해 주었으며 숲을 테라스 앞까지 들여와 철따라 피는 야생화의 흐드러짐이 이루어내는 자연과의 조화를 보여주었다.

그 사이로 소로길과 작은 쉼터만 내어 준 소박한 디자인을 구상해 보았으며 이곳에서는 5월의 좋은날 주말 오후엔 테라스 앞 넓은 잔디마당에서 하얀 웨딩드레스의 신부라도 볼 수 있는, 오후 음악회의 감미로운 선율까지도 기대해 볼 수 있으리라.

Bojung Daelim Village in Youngin-si is a typical rural type suburbicarian housing area in which you can freely meet the green bush that hugs this area; clean mountain stream that flows down between the feet of mountain; green field that spreads out between expressways; and whispering wind.

Topographically, this area is an around 10% slope in overall, which does not have plane land big enough to be used except for some paved part. We, therefore, made a water space where 2 mountain streams flow down into this housing complex through the terraced flowerbed by harmonization with the topography, the stream water gathers to make a quick rise and drop. We pulled the bush out to the front of the terrace to show the harmonization with the nature that is made by the blossoming of the wild plants.

We simply designed this pulled-out bush making a narrow path and a small arbor in it, which makes you expect to see a bride in a white wedding dress on the spacious grass field in front of the terrace on a good day of weekends in May and to hear a luscious melody.

▲Entrance plaza

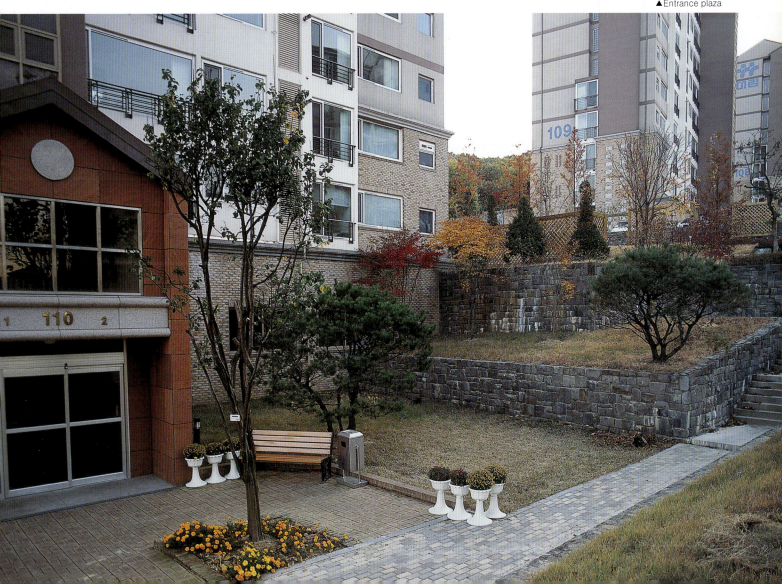

▲▼Promenade

▲Wood deck

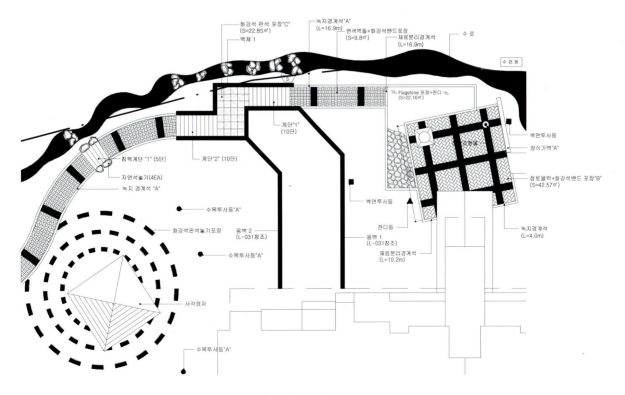

화강석 판석 포장"C"
(S=22.85㎡)

벽체 1

녹지경계석"A"
(L=16.9m)

변색벽돌+화강석밴드포장
(S=9.8㎡)

재료분리경계석
(L=16.9m)

수 로

수련원

Flagstone 포장+잔디
(S=22.16㎡)

계단"1"
(10단)

벽면투사등

장식가벽"A"

점토블럭+화강석밴드 포장"B"
(S=42.57㎡)

계단"2" (10단)

침목계단 "1" (5단)

자연석놀기(4EA)

녹지 경계석"A"

수목투사등"A"

화강석판석놀기포장

옹벽 2
(L-031참조)

수목투사등"A"

사각정자

수목투사등"A"

벽면투사등

옹벽 1
(L-031참조)

재료분리경계석
(L=10.2m)

잔디등

녹지경계석
(L=4.0m)

Part plan - Bamboo grove

▲Grass stairway

▲Putting green

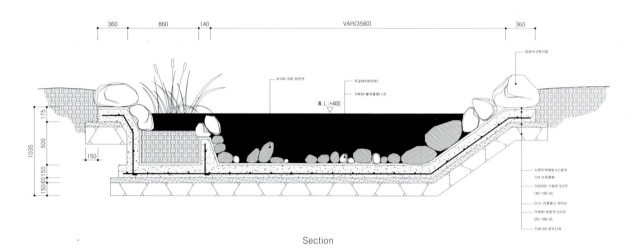

Section

▲Fountain

▲워터 플라자
눈으로만보는 수(水) 공간이 아닌 만질수 있고 개울에서 물장구치듯 발 아래로 흐르는 물을 접할 수 있는 분수로 계획, 새로운 개념의 참여적 공간으로 마련하였다.

▲Water plaza
A participating space of a new concept was arranged, not a water space that only offers visibility, but a senctioned square that one can feel the water flows below his/her feet as if paddling in it.

▲Pathway▼Fountain

▲Landscape art

▲Wall fountain

▲Water plaza▼Fountain

조경설계 : (주)성호엔지니어링 (02)566-9996
건축설계 : (주)일진종합건축사사무소
조경시공 : (주)수림조경산업＋아세아환경조경
위　　치 : 서초구 잠원동 50번지 외
대지면적 : 11,936.60 ㎡
조경면적 : 4,133.70 ㎡
건 폐 율 : 19.86 %
용 적 률 : 312.45 %

Landscape Design : Sungho Engineering Co., Ltd.
Architect Design : Iljin architecture &
　　　　　　　　　　Engineers Co,. Ltd.
Construction : Sulim Landscape Co., Ltd.＋
　　　　　　　　Asia Environment Landscape
Site Area : 11,936.60㎡
Landscape Area : 4,133.70㎡
Building Coverage Ratio : 19.86%
Floor Area Ratio : 312.45%

▲Promenade

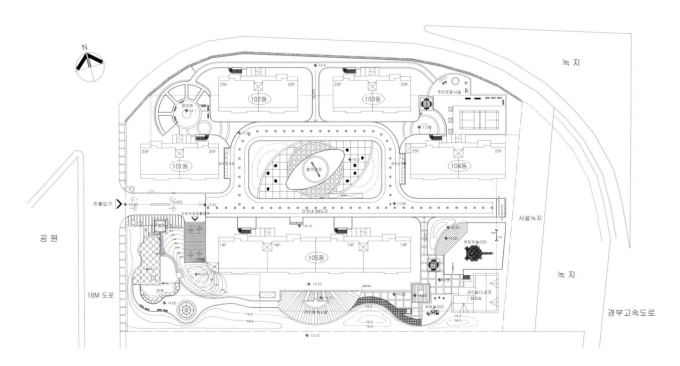

Master plan

▲Pathway

공간의 단절을 최소화하며 조형성과 자연성이 어우러진 아름다운 주거공간으로 자리 잡은 단지 '잠원동 롯데캐슬 갤럭시'는 주변 경관과 부합되는 최대한의 녹지 확보와 휴게공간의 조성, 공원속의 아파트라는 컨셉하에 중세 유럽의 장식요소와 고급스러운 소재들을 사용해 고급화의 이미지를 추구하였다. 쾌적한 주거공간을 창출하기 위해 계절의 변화를 즐길 수 있는 조망을 만들어 주며 이웃주민과 함께 할 수 있는 다양한 공간을 연출, 그 공간마다 차별성 있는 공간으로 만드는데 주력해 지루하지 않은 따스한 공간으로 자리잡길 기대한다.

전정 - 기억의 샘(로툰다), 장미터널, 소나무 데크
　　　(Pine Deck), 유아·어린이 놀이공간 등 ;
　　　캐슬에 대한 상상유도
중정 - 중앙광장 조형분수, 소나무, 자연석 의자
후정 - 장미원, 소나무기르 단풍터널, 휘트니스코스

'Jamwon Complex of Lotte Castle Galaxy' is a beautiful housing complex harmonizing the formativeness and naturalness minimizing the discontinuance of the space. Therefore, we designed the landscape of this complex focusing on securing the green filed and resting place as much as possible and using luxurious materials to make luxurious images. In order to make more comfortable housing complex, we designed various spaces from which you could enjoy the change of season and in which you could make communities with the neighbors. All these spaces are distinguished from each other with its own color, so we hope they can become warming spaces that are not boring.

Front Garden - Fount of Memory (Rotunda), Tunnel of Rose, Pine Deck, Infants · Children's Playground and etc. ; Inducing the image of castle

Middle Garden - Art Fountain of Central Square, Pine, Nature Stone Chair

Rear Garden - Rose Garden, Pine Road with Maple Tree Tunnel, Fitness Course

▲Pathway▼Playground

▲Promenade

▲Resting place ▼Landscape arts

I-Space, Bundang

조경설계 : 기술사 사무소 아텍 (02)567-0841
건축설계 : 현대산업개발(주)
시　공 : 현대산업개발(주)
위　치 : 경기도 성남시 분당구
대지면적 : 1단지 - 17,241.10㎡, 2단지 - 7,035.50㎡
녹지면적 : 1단지 - 3,45192㎡, 2단지 - 1,419.06㎡
세 대 수 : 1단지 - 540세대 (지하 3층 ~지상 34층)
　　　　　 2단지 - 224세대 (지하 3층~지상 31층)

Landscape Design : ARTEC
Architecture Design : Hyundai Development Company
Construction : Hyundai Development Company
Site Area : 1 Block-17,241.10㎡, 2 Block - 7,035.50㎡
Green Area : 1 Block-3,45192㎡, 2 Block-1,419.06㎡
Household : 1 Block-540 Families, (B3F~34F)
　　　　　　 2 Block-224 Families, (B3F~31F)

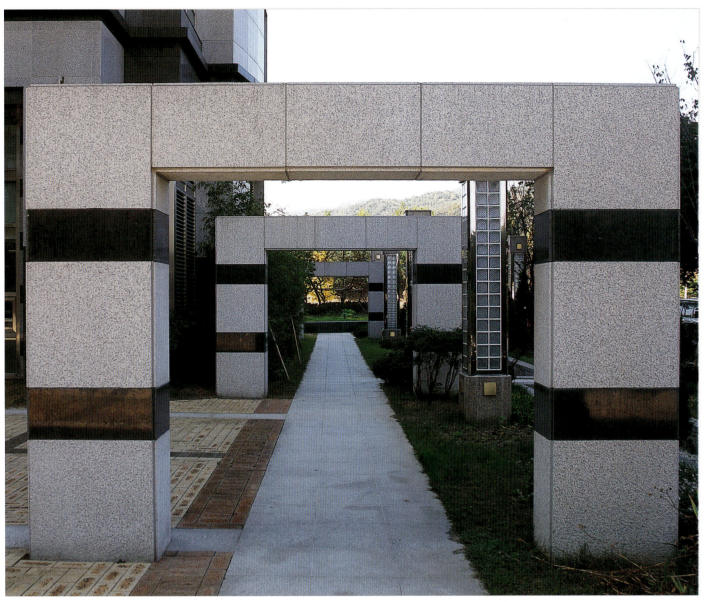

▲Pathway

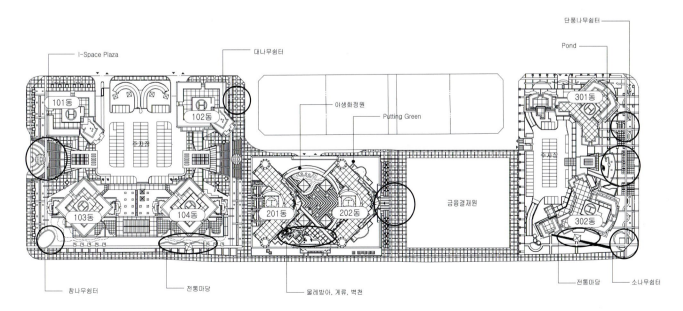

Master plan

▲Fountain

경기도 성남시 분당구에 위치한 'I-Space'는 고대 로마시대에 세워진 신전인 '판테온'을 모티브로 디자인 하였다. 판테온을 모티브로 자연적인 요소(물, 야생화 화류, 바위 등)들을 적극적으로 도입, 물은 수로를 통한 다양하고 특화된 공간을 연출하였으며 야생화와 자연석들은 조화롭게 배치되어 자연미를 강조해 주었다. 체계적인 조명계획을 통해 야간의 이용자들을 배려하는 분위기를 조성해 주는 것도 빼놓지 않았다. 건물 우측으로는 보행자를 배려한 보행전용 통로를 조성하고 조명 열주 등의 설치와 야생화단지와 벤치를 배치해 보행로 내 휴게기능 및 경관성을 높이고자 하였다.

1층 지상부의 공간적 협소함을 극복하기 위해 3층 옥상부를 활용하여 공간을 조성하였으며 이 공간은 단지주민의 체력을 단련 할 수 있는 공간으로 제공된다. 광장을 위요하는 형태의 녹지대 조성, 부드러운 마운딩 및 경관석의 도입, 야생화의 군락형성은 자연스러운 경관을 조성해주며 단지 후면부에 조형 연식의자를 배치하여 단지민 및 인근 보행자의 휴게장소로 만들어 주었다. 또한 경관성 향상을 위해 덩굴 장미등 만경류 식재와 함께한 등의자의 배치로 보는것이 즐거운 휴게 공간으로 계획 하였다.

외부의 위험요소로부터 어린이들을 보호하고 아늑한 공간을 조성하기 위하여 원형의 가벽을 설치, 도시에 지반을 고려 경량 놀이시설도 함께 설치하였다. 강한 바람에 직접 노출된 악조건을 고려하여 나무갑판, 낙엽관목 및 지피화초류에 의한 공간 계획과 입주민들을 위한 외부경관 조망, 명상을 위한 티 라운지 성격의 공간도 함께 조성하였다.

Located in Bundang of Sungnam, Kyunggi-province, I-space is borrowed its design from the early Roman shrine, Pantheon. The natural elements, mainly water, wildflowers, rocks and etc, are introduced to show its motif from Pantheon. Water is designed to produce the diverse and peculiar space through waterways. With the wildflowers rocks are arranged to focus on the natural beauty by displaying them in harmony. For the pedestrians at night the designers could not forget the systemic lights. On the right of building you can see the greenways, wildflower beds and bench to make people feel at home.

To overcome the space limit the designers would like to make the advantage of 3rd floor's rooftop. Consequently, this widened space is offered to villagers for physical training. By making green zones and mounding, introducing the landscape rocks and displaying the wildflower beds people can enjoy the natural beauty. People also can take a rest on a serial bench placed at the backside of building and this serial bench is placed at the high of the eyes considering the exterior. Potted vine plants such like climbing roses with rattan chairs it will be regarded as the best place for resting.

Children can be protected by building the tentative wall and it will make people feel homey. In this place you can see the playground for children. Considering the strong wind the designers would like to implant the shrubs and plants covering soil surface to foster a space for the exterior as well as a lounge for villagers.

▲Fountain

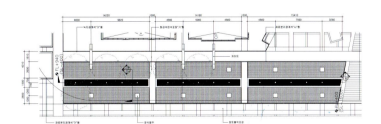

Top - view

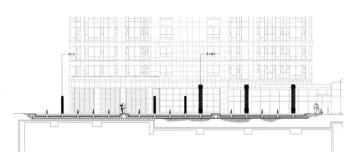

Elevation

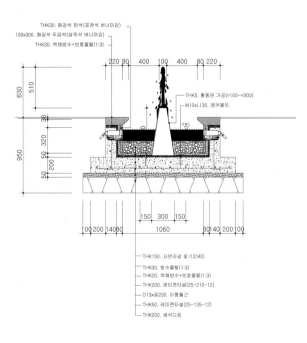

Section

▲Sketch – Colonade

▲Sketch – Promenade

▲Sketch – Water facilities (water mill → torrent → wall fountain → pond)

▲▼Courtyard

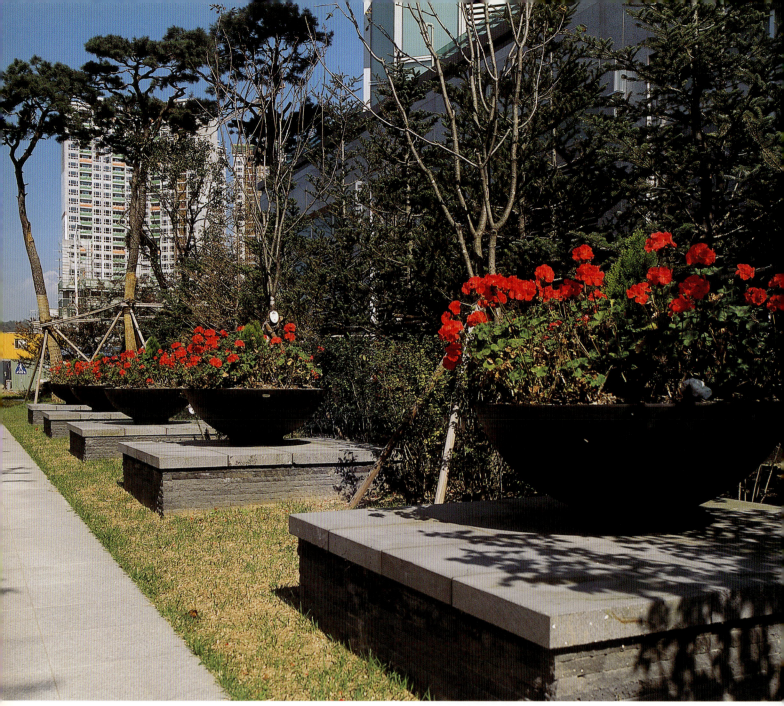

▲Planter bowl

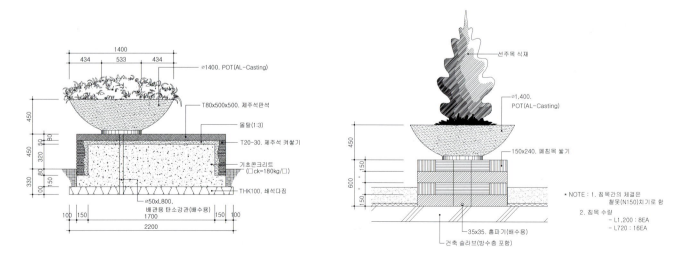

1400
434　533　434

∅1400. POT(AL-Casting)

T80x500x500. 제주석판석

몰탈(1:3)

T20-30. 제주석 켜쌓기

기초콘크리트
(□ck=180kg/□)

THK100. 쇄석다짐

450

450

50 80

330 150 320 80

∅50xL800.
배관용 탄소강관(배수용)
100 150 1700 150 100
2200

선주목 식재

∅1,400.
POT(AL-Casting)

150x240. 폐침목 쌓기

450

600 150 150

35x35. 출파기(배수용)

건축 슬라브(방수층 포함)

• NOTE : 1. 침목간의 체결은
철못(N150)치기로 함
2. 침목 수량
- L1,200 : 8EA
- L720 : 16EA

Elevation & Section

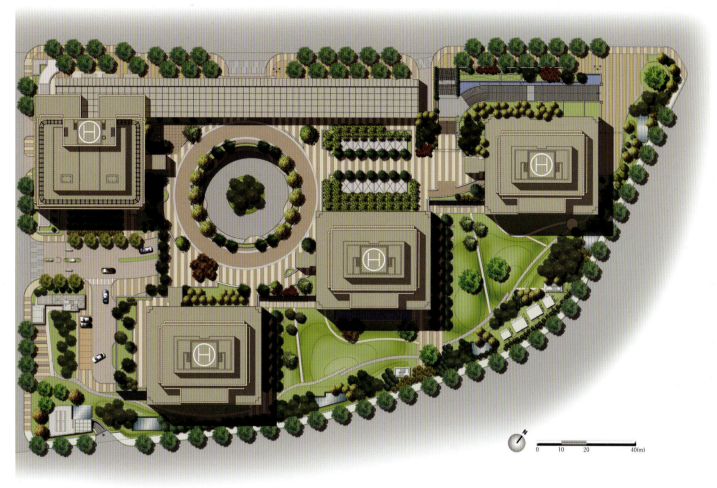

Master plan

■ Landscape design concept Ⅰ, Ⅱ

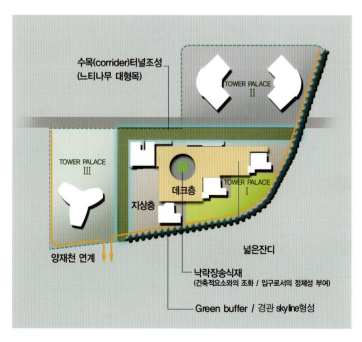

수목(corrider)터널조성
(느티나무 대형목)

TOWER PALACE
Ⅱ

TOWER PALACE
Ⅲ

데크층

지상층

TOWER PALACE
Ⅰ

양재천 연계

넓은잔디

낙락장송식재
(건축적요소와의 조화 / 입구로서의 정체성 부여)

Green buffer / 경관 skyline형성

지배적 건축요소와의 조화

분리된 부지의 일체감 조성

Green Layer 2

Green Layer 1

양재천과의 공간적 연계

조경설계 : SWA+(주)삼성애버랜드 (02)6230-3031
건축설계 : 삼우설계
시　　공 : (주)삼성애버랜드
위　　치 : 서울특별시 강남구 도곡동 467번지
대지면적 : 33,696.10㎡
조경면적 : 8,926.55㎡

Landscape Design : SWA+Samsung Everland Inc.
Architecture Design : Samoo Architects & Engineers
Construction : Samsung Everland Inc.
Site Area : 33,696.10㎡
Landscape Area : 8,926.55㎡

▲▼Entrance

▲Pathway

▲▼Pathway

양재천이 주변으로 있는 도곡동 타워팰리스는 그 이점을 이용, 단지 전체 혹은 개별단지가 조깅로와 산책로를 통해 양재천과 연결된다.

위치상 도로에 의해 공간적, 시각적으로 분리된 3개의 부지가 오히려 조경의 구성요소로 사용되어 경관적, 기능적으로 보다 밀착되고 일체감을 갖도록 해주며 도로에 강한 계절감을 가지는 대형목(느티나무)을 식재하고 보도에는 특별한 색감을 가진 포장재료를 사용하여 강한 공간의 특색을 표현해 주었다. 차도의 특별한 포장재 도입은 개별단지 사이의 연계성을 강조하고 차량속도 완화의 효과를 보여준다.

보도에는 가로수, 포장과 함께 전체적으로 디자인된 의자를 배치하여 단지주민과 외부인들과의 이용 편의성을 고려해 주며 전체 단지의 입구는 환경조형물 등을 조명과 함께 조화롭게 배치하여 게이트웨이(gate way)의 이미지를 부여해 주었다. 단지 안에서만의 조경이 아닌 주변으로의 확장된 조경계획으로 정해져있는 공간에서 벗어나 더 확 트인 조경공간을 제공, 답답한 도시에 마음껏 숨을 내쉴 수 있는 공간으로 남길 기대한다.

Tower Palace in Dokok-dong takes an advantage of the surrounding Yangjaecheon thus liking its individual or whole units to the stream through the walking & jogging paths.

The site, though it is divided into three sections by roads because of its location, only provides adhering and unifying feeling, as a landscape component, in scenic and functional sides. Strongness of the space was represented by planting large-sided trees (zelkova) of seasonal sense on the road and on sidewalks, using paving materials, which has a distinctive color sense. Introduction of the special paving material emphasized the connection among the individual units, and also shows effectiveness in decrease of the vehicle's speed.

On the sidewalk, along with the street tree and the pavement, the designed benches offer convenience to residents and guests. The main entrance of the apartment blocks produces an image of a gateway in harmony with landscape architectures and illuminations. Planning not only the landscape inside the blocks, but one expanded to the surroundings, it provides clearer and wider landscape beyond the arranged space. So it can be a place that one feels free in a stuffy city.

▲Pathway ▼Promenade

부천 상동 서해그랑블 (8, 12블럭)

조경설계 : (주)우리엔 디자인펌 (02)572-3168
건축설계 : (주)티씨엠씨 건축사사무소
시   공 : (주)서해종합건설
위   치 : 부천상동
대지면적 : 8블럭 − 31,953㎡, 12블럭 − 27,820㎡
조경면적 : 8블럭 − 111,618.57㎡, 12블럭 − 9,886.74㎡
세 대 수 : 8블럭 − 454 세대, 12블럭 − 402 세대

Landscape Design : Uri Design Firm
Architecture Design : TCMC Architects & Engineers
Construction : Seohai Construction Co., Ltd.
Site Area : 8 Block − 31,953㎡, 12 Block − 27,820㎡
Landscape Area : 8 Block − 111,618.57㎡,
          12 Block − 9,886.74㎡
Household : 8 Block − 454 Families,
          12 Block − 402 Families

▲Resting place (12BL)

'행복한 마을'이라는 단지 이름을 가진 이곳은 주민의 이용과 편익을 도모하는 것 이상으로 지역사회에서의 공공성을 중시하여 외부공간을 계획, 배치하였다. 도로변에 녹지, 파고라, 연식의자로 이루어진 선형의 공개공지를 조성하여 주민과 외부인이 모두 이용할 수 있는 공공의 공간으로 만들었고, 단지 남측으로는 보행통로를 조성하여 단지 서쪽의 보행자도로에서 단지 동쪽의 도로로 통하는 동선 역할을 할 수 있도록 계획하였다.

이 보행통로는 차량의 통행을 전면 금지한 순수 보행통로로서 녹음수인 느티나무를 열식하여 그늘을 제공하고, 곳곳에 배드민턴장, 파고라와 의자를 설치하여 운동과 휴게의 기능을 더하였다.

단지 남북과 동서를 가르는 동선의 중심에 자리한 중앙광장에는 휴게공간의 기능이 강한 팔각정과 야외무대의 설치로 사람들간의 활동성을 높여주었으며 어린이놀이터, 농구장, 화훼원은 하나의 공간으로 계획되어 다양한 연령대의 사람들이 함께 할 수 있도록 해주었다.

Since this complex name is 'a happy village', we planned to design the outside space focusing on the public nature of the local community not less than on seeking the use and convenience of the residents.

At the roadside, we made a linear open public area that consisted of green field, pergola and benches so that the residents and visitors could use this area altogether. At the southern side of this complex, we designed a walkway that could play the role of moving-line from the pedestrian road located at the western side of this complex through to the road located at the eastern side of this complex. Along this walkway that is a pure walkway to which the cars are prohibited entering, zelkovas and trees are planted to provide shadow. In this space, we also disposed badminton ground, pergola and chairs to mix the athletic and resting function. In the central square located on the center of the moving-line that only divides the direction into the south and north and into the east and west, we constructed an octagonal pavilion and open stage to enhance the active nature of the residents. The children's playground, basketball court and botanical garden were designed to be in a space so that all aged people could enjoy themselves altogether in this space.

▲Sports facilities (8BL)

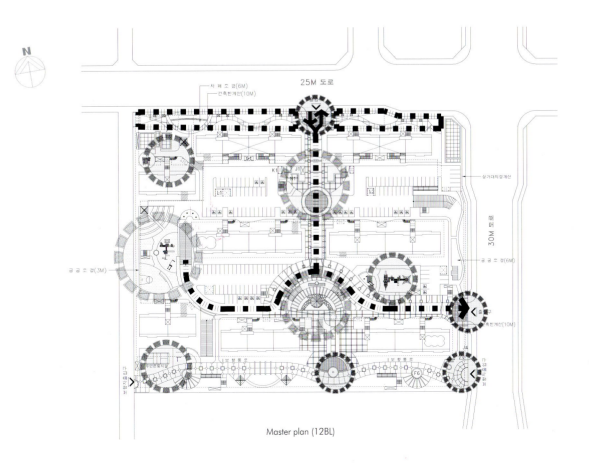

Master plan (12BL)

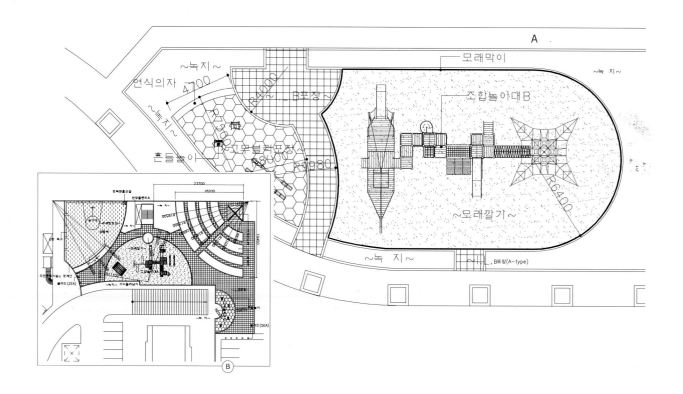

Part plan

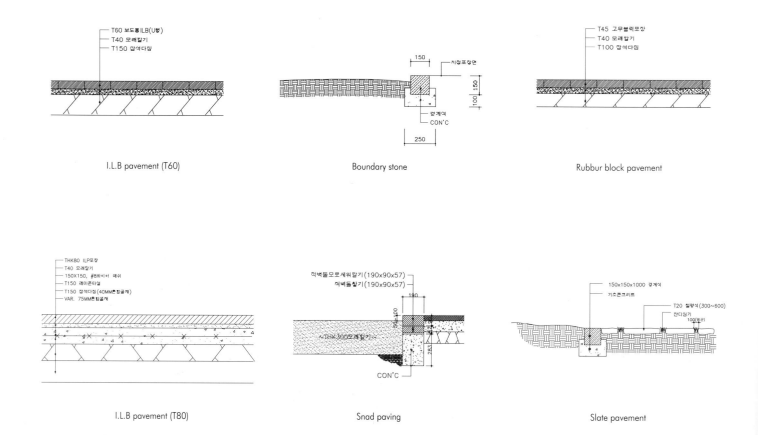

I.L.B pavement (T60)

Boundary stone

Rubbur block pavement

I.L.B pavement (T80)

Snad paving

Slate pavement

▲▼Playground (12BL)

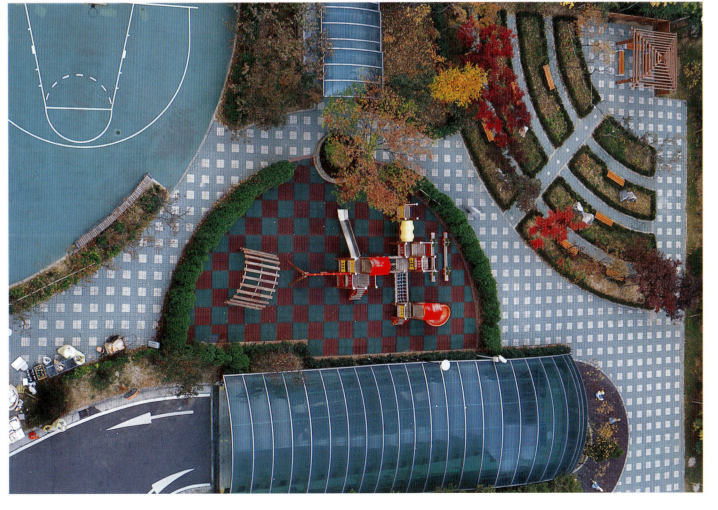

▲▼Pathway (8BL)

▲Pathway 8BL▼Pathway12BL

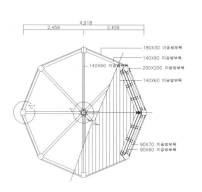

Floor plan

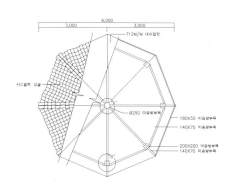

Ceiling plan

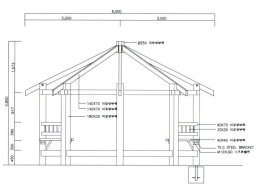

Elevation

▲Gate(12BL)

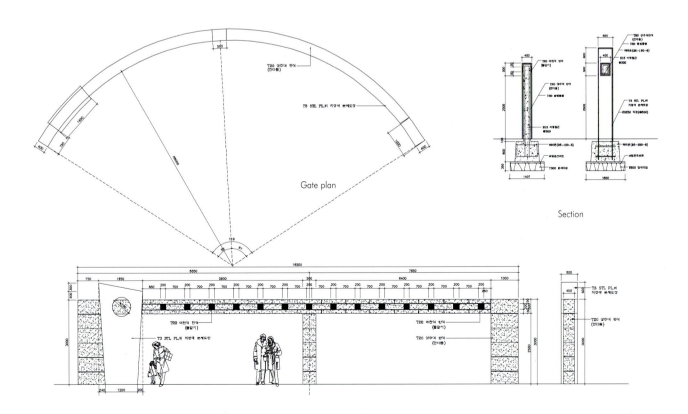

Gate plan

Section

Elevation

▲Space frame(12BL)

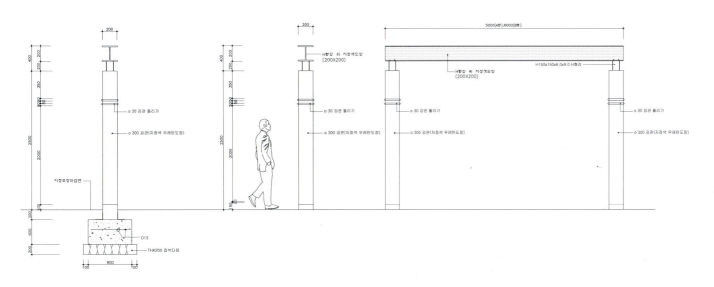

Section   Side view   Front view

조경설계 : 기술사사무소 아텍 (02)567-0841
조경시공 : 두성조경(주)
위   치 : 서울시 강남구 대치동 970번지
대지면적 : 9,865.10㎡
조경면적 : 2,073.69㎡

Landscape Design : ARTEC Landscape Design
Landscape Construction : Doosung Landscape
                         Architecture
Site Area : 9,865.10㎡
Landscape Area : 2,073.69㎡

▲▼Waterway

▲Pathway

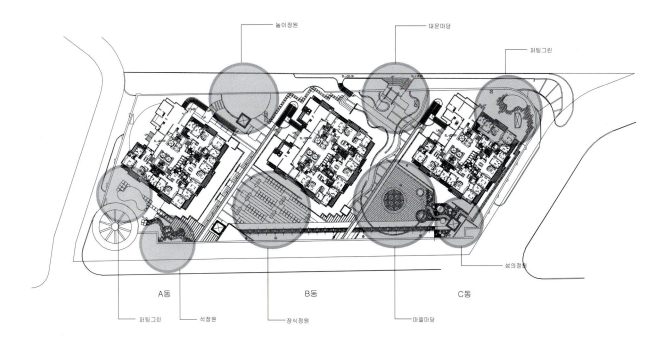

Master plan

▲Sketch – Entrance gate

풍부한 녹지축에서 안정된 정서를 기반으로 보다 긴밀한 유대감 증대를 도모하고자 '그린 커뮤니티' 공간을 만들어 조형적 아름다움의 녹지 경관을 연출하고자 하였다.

바다를 주제로 한 수경연출기법을 도입하였으며 다양한 시각방향을 고려한 배치계획 및 바다로의 조망을 배려한 식재 계획과 전망공간을 수립하였다.

부지의 입지적 성격을 고려한 공간 및 디자인 패턴 도입과 자갈 정원, 섬의 정원, 파도 정원 등의 명확한 컨셉을 제시하였다.

Based on the plentiful green zones the beauty of the green is emphasized to produce closer ties between the villagers by making 'the green community'. Introducing the water culture techniques with a motif borrowed from the sea and considering the diverse optic angles the designers had to find out what the most suitable arrangement of plants and space for fine views of the sea. In the process the designers offered the pebble garden, the island garden and the wave garden to show their definite concept for the space and design took a consideration of its location

▲Sketch – Community plaza & Pond

▲Sketch – Stone garden

▲Resting place▼Landscape arts

▲Granite stepston path

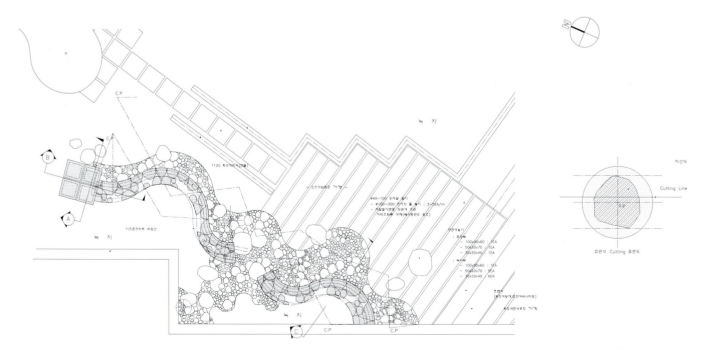

Part plan

▲Granite stepstone path

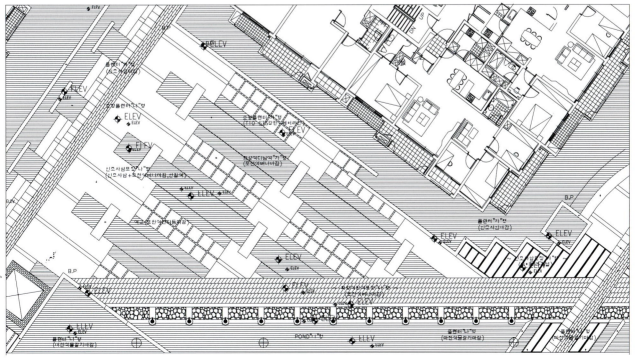

Part plan

▲Community plaza

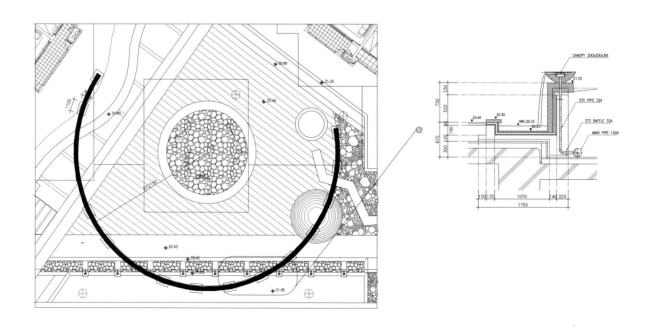

Part plan

▲Community plaza

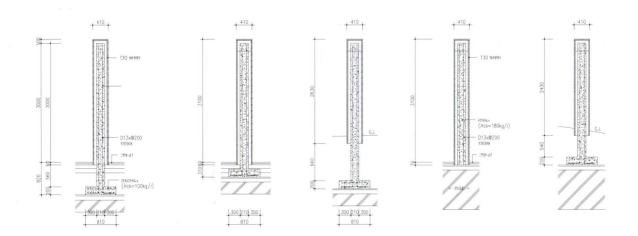

Section detail

Part plan

▲Deck

조경설계 : (주)성호엔지니어링 (02)566-9996
건축설계 : 종합건축사사무소 세일
시   공 : (주)푸른공간
위   치 : 서초구 방배동 888-34
조경면적 : A동−434.6㎡, B동−500.8㎡, C동−203.7㎡
세 대 수 : 57세대

Landscape Design : Sungho Engineering Co., Ltd.
Architecture Design : Architecture group seil
Construction : Green Space Co., Ltd.
Landscape Area : A Buildings−434.6㎡,
                 B Buildings−500.8㎡,
                 C Buildings−203.7㎡
Household : 57 Families

▲Granite stepstone path

방배동 롯데 캐슬파크는 외부와는 차별성을 띤 고급스런 소재와 사계절 푸른 상록수 식재들이 주는 포근한 색감을 이용하여 공간의 한곳 한곳을 마치 여인이 하얀 천위에 자수를 놓듯 차분하게 하나하나 풀어놓은 곳이다. 주민들의 친밀한 유대관계 형성과 친환경적인 공간 창출이란 다소 진부적이지만 도시생활에서 가장 필요한 논제를 가지고 공간을 형성해 주었으며 협소한 공간이라는 불안적인 요소를 완화시켜주기 위해서 친환경적인 포장재를 사용해 설계 하였다.

관목과 둥근소나무 조형소나무를 이용해 스카이라인을 조성한 그린가든은 시각적인 개방감을 주며 곳곳에 티 테이블을 배치함으로써 주민들의 상호 작용의 기회를 제공하게 된다.

단아한 한국의 선을 이용해 '물의정원Ⅰ'을 조성하였으며 '물의정원Ⅱ'는 강한 유럽풍의 정원으로 '물의정원Ⅰ'과는 같은 성격의 공간이면서도 서로 상이한 공간으로 표현하였다. 특히, '물의정원Ⅱ'는 화강석의 웅장한 벽면과 자연적 지형이 주는 단차를 이용한 조형미가 돋보이는 벽천, 그리고 토피아리 식재패턴을 강하게 표출한 공간이다.

바닥의 패턴은 문라이트(moon light)란 주재를 따뜻한 소재인 점토벽돌과 고급스런 화강석을 이용하여 표현함으로써 품격있는 단지를 조성하였다.

조망데크는 주민들의 유대관계를 위해 휴게 공간을 한정하여 집약시킨 공간으로 호석의 플랜터와 상록수가 주는 안정감 있는 위요감, 필로티에 의해 형성되는 입구구성은 주민들간의 친밀한 유대관계 형성에 좋은 계기를 마련해 주기에 적합한 공간이라 생각한다.

Used the distinctive high-grade materials and the color senses of evergreen trees, this apartment reminds people with woman who does embroidery on white cloth. As the basic theme for the city life was thought to have the close ties between the neighbors and to use the eco-friendly materials, it was used to pro-environment materials to soften the instability caused by the narrowness of space.

The green zones which are made of the shrubs and pine trees give people optic openness and the tea table arranged several places to offer the villagers the chances to improve their interpersonal communications.

'The water park I' that used the Korean elegance line has both similarity and difference with 'the water park II' that is decorated by the way of European style. '

The water park II', especially is the space where the plants are potted in artificial and its landscape is eminent. With the wall fountain people can appreciate the splendid outlook of granites.

To express the elegance of the building the designer used the granites and bricks to the bottom space.

The villagers can feel the stability which is given by the rock planters and evergreen trees at the view deck. Moreover the entrance formed by the pilotis is good enough for the communities and contributes closer ties among the villagers.

▲Granite stepstone path

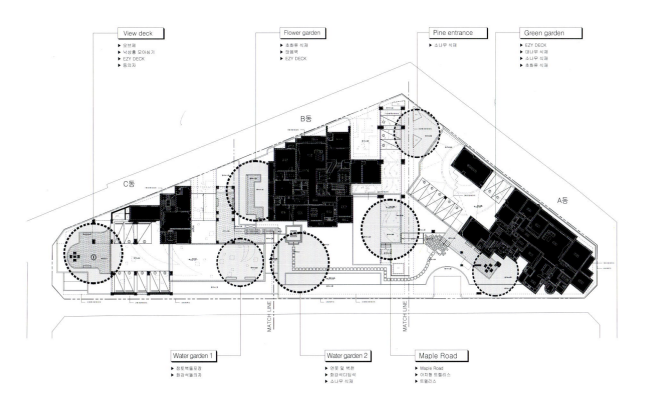

View deck	Flower garden	Pine entrance	Green garden
▶ 오브제	▶ 초화류 식재	▶ 소나무 식재	▶ EZY DECK
▶ 낙상홍 모아심기	▶ 앗물벽		▶ 대나무 식재
▶ EZY DECK	▶ EZY DECK		▶ 소나무 식재
▶ 등의자			▶ 초화류 식재

B동

C동

A동

MATCH LINE

MATCH LINE

Water garden 1	Water garden 2	Maple Road
▶ 점토벽돌포장	▶ 연못 및 벽천	▶ Maple Road
▶ 화강석의자	▶ 화강석디딤석	▶ 아치형 트렐리스
	▶ 소나무 식재	▶ 트렐리스

Master plan

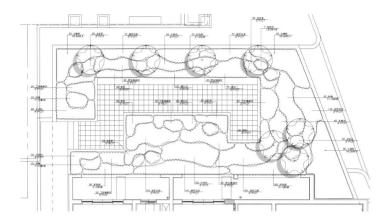

Part plan

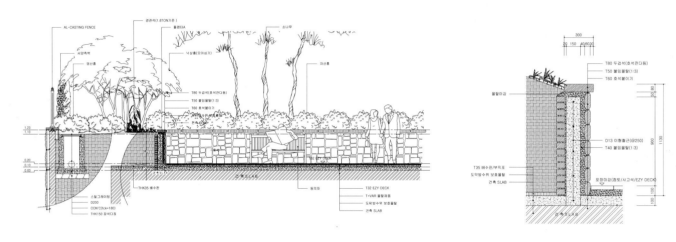

Section

Section detail (planter-A)

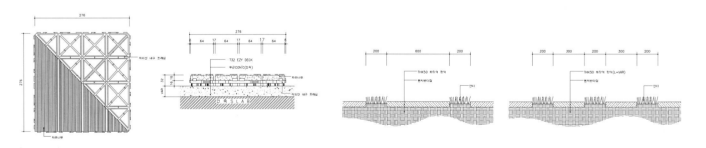

Ezy deck detail

Granite stepstone A, B

Granite plate

Sagosuk(Granite) Pavement

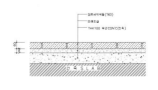

Clay brick pavement

▲Entrance court▼Wall fountain

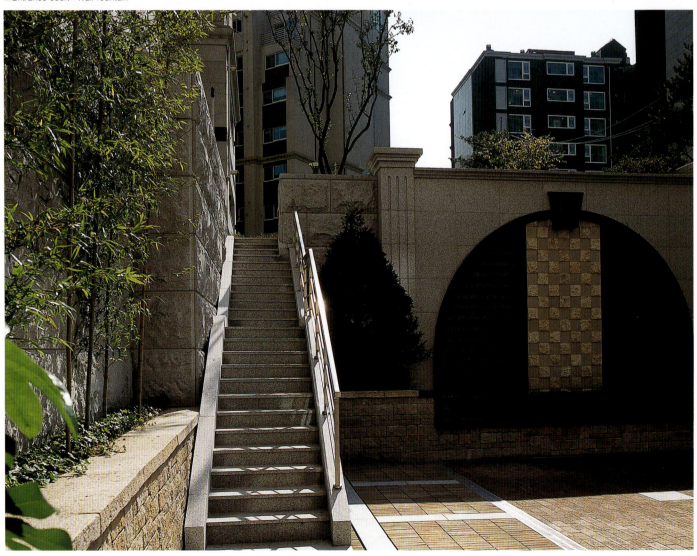

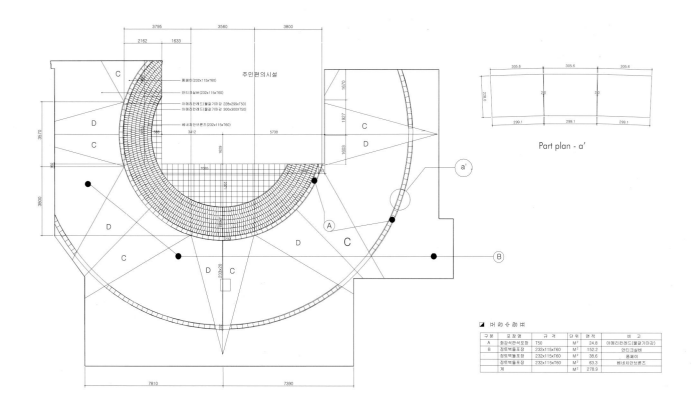

Part plan

Part plan - a'

구분	포장명	규 격	단위	면적	비 고
A	화강석판석포장	T50	M²	24.8	아메리칸레드(물갈기마감)
B	점토벽돌포장	232x115xT60	M²	152.2	안티크실버
	점토벽돌포장	232x115xT60	M²	38.6	폼페이
	점토벽돌포장	232x115xT60	M²	63.3	베네치안브론즈
	계		M²	278.9	

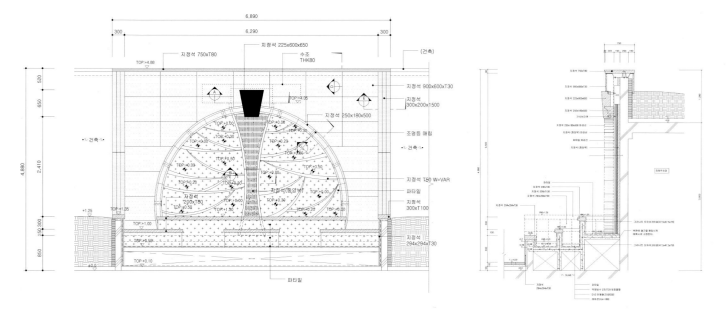

Elevation

Section - A

Samsung 5-cha Apartment, Suji

조경 기본계획 : 바인플랜 + 하셀 (홍콩)
조경 기본 · 실시 설계 : 바인플랜 · 윤미방 (02)3413-0898
시   공 : (주)삼성물산 주택부문 조경팀
조경식재 : 두성조경 + 고은조경
색채계획 : 한양대학교 · 유희준 교수
위   치 : 경기도 용인시 풍덕천리 215-8
면   적 : 128.915㎡
세 대 수 : 1,828세대

Landscape Basic Plan : Vine Plan + Hassell (Hong Kong)
Landscape Basic · Execution Design : Vine Plan ·
                                        Yoon, Mi bang
Construction : Samsung corp.
                   Construction& Development
Landscape Planting : Doosung Landscape Architecture +
                          Goun Landscape Architecture
Color Plan : You, Hee jun · Prof. of Hanyang Univ.
Site Area : 128.915㎡
Green Area : 40,100.78㎡
Household : 1,828 Families

▲Entrance

▲Promenade

Master plan

주변의 기존 야산과 연계될 수 있도록 원형보전 녹지를 비롯한 단지 주변의 산책로는 최대한 자연친화적 공간으로 조성하고, 중앙광장을 비롯한 곳곳의 조경공간은 최대한 이용자 위주의 공간으로 꾸며 계획하였다.

또한 실제 이용자들이 고층 아파트 단지에서 느끼기 쉬운 답답함을 조금이라도 해소할 수 있도록 여유 있는 공간으로 조성 하고자 하였다.

아파트 측면에는 대나무를 군식해서 산석과 조화로운 경관이 연출되며, 또 아파트 내, 쓰레기 분리수거함 주변에 산석을 쌓아 단지 전체의 이미지를 제고시켰다. 심지어 쓰레기 수거함은 물론이고, 주차장 상부에 과감하게 파고라를 설치함으로써 조금이라도 기존의 단지계획이 안고 있던 삭막함을 완화시키고자 하였다.

The original-condition-conserved green field and the walkway surrounding this whole complex were designed to be environmental friendly spaces so that they could be harmonized with the hills around, and the other landscaping sites including the central hall ground were designed focusing on the users of them as much as we could.

We made efforts to form a roomy space so that the actual users could ease their stress that they could easily get in the high-rise condominium complex.

Bamboos were planted at the side of this complex so that this complex could produce a sight harmonized with the hill stones, which were also piled up around the garbage-separate boxes in the condominium complex to enhance the whole image of this complex. Pergola were built not only around the garbage-separate boxes but also at the upper parts of the parking lot boldly in order to alleviate the dryness given by the previous plan for this complex as much as we could.

▲Sketch

▲Resting place

▲Promenade

Seocho Garden Suite

Master plan

조경설계 : 바인플랜 (02)3413-0898
시   공 : (주)삼성물산 주택부분 조경팀
위   치 : 서울특별시 서초구 서초동 1326번지
대지면적 : 13,341.00㎡
녹지면적 : 4,041.43㎡
세 대 수 : 141세대

Landscape Design : Vine Plan
Construction : Samsung Corp. Housing Dept.
              Landscape Div.
Site Area : 13,341.00㎡
Green Area : 4,041.43㎡
Household : 141 Families

서초 가든 스위트는 건물 내에 헬스, 골프, 조깅트랙 등 다양한 운동시설을 갖추고 있는 강남역 주변에 위치한 고층의 고품격 주거단지이다.

실내에 운동시설을 충분히 갖추고 있어 외부로는 산책, 휴식 등 자연을 만끽할 수 있는 공간 마련에 그 주안점을 두어 설계되어졌으며 요란한 장식을 배제하고 기능성을 위주로 한 미니멀한 디자인 개념으로 접근하였다.

식재계획은 형태가 자연스럽게 흐드러지는 수목과 자생화, 지피류 등을 식재하여 풍성한 자연의 이미지를 고조시킬 수 있도록 해주었으며 또 대형 소나무를 군식하여 소나무 숲 사이에서 건물이 솟아있는 분위기를 조성하였다.

더욱이 1층 전면의 유리면으로 된 선큰 내부로 소나무가 투영되어 실내까지 자연이 유입되도록 하여 사람들이 어느 공간에서건 항상 자연을 느낄 수 있도록 해주었다.

직선 처리의 수로는 주어진 공간 내에서 깊이감을 더해주는 요소로 이 공간의 끝에 하나의 가벽을 더해 공간의 연장감을 지속시켜 주었으며 가벽을 따라 떨어지는 물은 수로를 따라 얇은 수막을 형성, 산책로를 따라 잔잔히 흐르도록 만들었다.

Seocho Garden Suite located nearby Kangnam subway station is a high-rise luxury housing complex in which there are various kinds of athletic facilities including a fitness center, golf club, jogging track and etc inside the building. This housing complex has the indoor athletic facilities, so the landscape design of this complex was focused on securing the space where the residents could fully enjoy the nature outside taking a walk, rest and etc. In addition, the minimal design concept was selected focusing on the functionality without loud decoration.

We planted the trees that hang down their branches and leaves naturally, native flowers, ground covers and etc to emphasize the image of abundant nature. We planted also huge size pines to form the view as if the buildings rising up out of the pinewoods. Furthermore, these pines throw their image onto the glass-made sunken inside. That is, the nature can enter into the inner building, so that people can enjoy the nature at any place in the building.

The straight-linear type waterway is a factor that adds the feel of depth to the given space, at the end of which a temporary wall is installed in order to keep the feel of extension. The water after dropping along the temporary wall, slowly flows along the walkway forming thin water film.

▲Resting place ▼Playground

▲Resting place▼Promenade

▲Pathway

▲Water course

조경설계 : (주)그룹 · 한
위　　치 : 부산광역시 연제구 거제1동
　　　　　314번지
대지면적 : 331,273㎡
조경면적 : 100,270.56㎡ (대지면적의
　　　　　30.27%)
규　　모 : 7,374세대
공사기간 : 1998. 4 ~ 2001. 6 (39개월)

Landscape Design : Group · Han Co., Ltd.
Site Area : 331,273㎡
Landscape Area : 100,270.56㎡
　　　　　　　　(30.27% of site area)
Building Scope : 7,374 Households
Construction Period : 1998. 4 ~ 2001. 6
　　　　　　　　　　(39 month)

▲Fountain

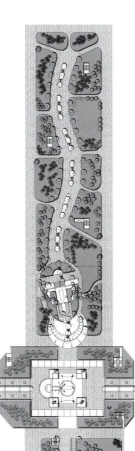

Bird's-eye view

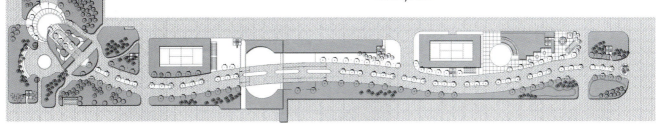

Master plan

▲Playground

▲Playground

Daelim (World Town) e-Pyeonhan Sesang, Sungsan

조경설계 : (주)동심원 · 안계동, 배민호 (02)544-5674
건축설계 : 대림산업(주)
조경시설물 : 청우개발
조경식재 : (주)고운조경
위　　치 : 서울시 마포구 성산동 148번지
대지면적 : 31,299㎡
녹지면적 : 9,854㎡
세대수 : 795세대(10개동)

Landscape Design : Dongsimwon Inc. ·
　　　　　　　　　　Ahn, Gyeo dong / Bae, Min ho
Architecture Design : Daelim Industrial Co.,Ltd.
Landscape Facilities : Cheong-woo Co., Ltd.
Landscape Planting : Goun Landscape Architecture
Site Area : 31,299㎡
Green Area : 9,854㎡
Household : 795 Families (10 Buildings)

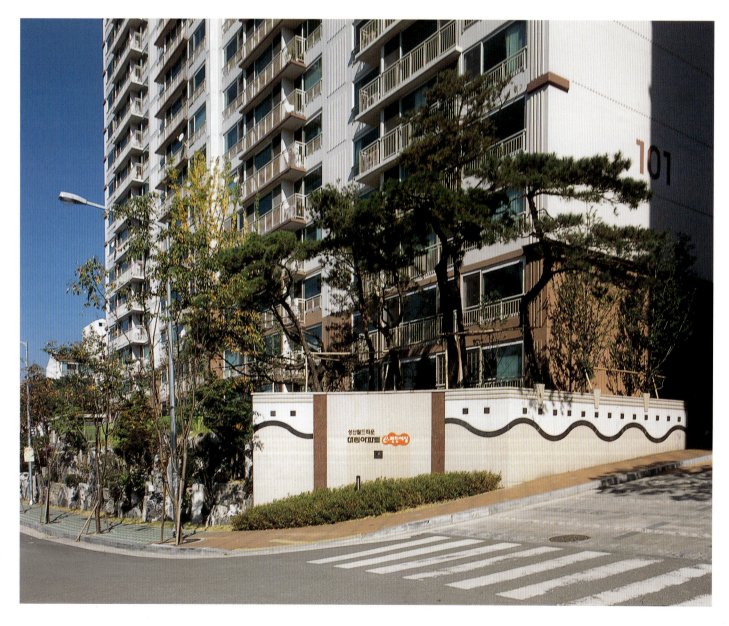

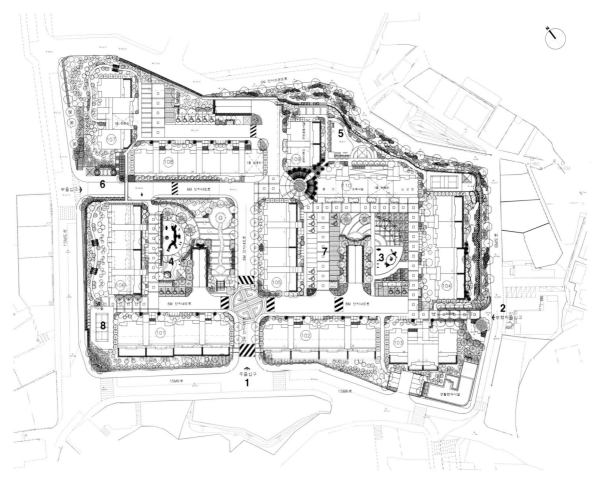

Master plan

2002년 월드컵의 개최로 주위 변화가 많았던 마포구 성산동에 위치한 이 단지는 상암 월드컵경기장이 손에 닿을 듯이 보이고, '하늘공원'과 '월드컵공원'이 가까이 위치하고 있다는 것만으로도 충분한 매력이 있는 곳이다. 이곳의 부출입구는 도로와 단지의 레벨차로 인해 형성되는 단차를 이용하여 벽천을 조성, 자연적인 재료와 산석, 목재 물레방아를 사용하여 따스하고 정겨운 느낌을 주었다. 이곳과는 반대로 주출입구는 세련되면서도 주위와 조화로운 분위기를 연출하고 있으며 교차로의 햇살무늬 포장패턴은 차량들이 나아갈 수 있는 방향을 보여주며 동선을 자연스럽게 유도한다.

머무르며 바라볼 수 있는 여유로움의 공간으로는 '노을의 정원', '아침의 정원'이라고 명명한 어린이 놀이터가 있다. 진입로를 통과하여 경사지의 끝에 오르면 도달하는 노을의 정원은 작은 조각물과 녹음수가 보이는 작은 쉼터이며 오며가며 쉴 수 있는 정거장 같은 곳이다.

아침의 정원 또한 휴게공간과 놀이공간의 완벽한 조화를 보여주는 곳으로 분수와 함께 만들어진 놀이터에서는 아이들이 뛰어노는 모습을 데크 위에 조성된 2단의 목재 플랜터에서 흐뭇하게 바라볼 수 있다.

만약 단지전체를 돌아보고 싶은 사람이 있다면 산책로가 시작되는 곳만 알려주면 된다. 산책로에 접어들면 공간과 공간을 연계하여 조성되어 있는 길을 따라 텃밭과 만나기도 하고, 농구장에서 운동하고 있는 아이들을 만날 수도 있다. 더욱이 산책로의 지압보도와 텃밭 같은 아기자기한 공간 설계는 주민들간의 대화를 도모해주며 이 공간은 아파트전체를 돌아볼 수 있는 공간이기에 산책이라는 목적 이외에 사람과 사람이 만나 정을 나눌 수 있는 커뮤니티의 장으로 이용된다.

This complex located in Sungsan-dong, Mapo-gu where there have been a lot of changes thanks to 2002 World Cup is attractive enough with only the fact that 'Sky Park' and 'World Cup Park' are nearby. At the sub-gate of this complex, we constructed a wall stream by using the bump (one of week points of this complex) that was formed by the level difference between the road and the complex, and we decorated this wall stream with the naturalistic materials such as hill stones, wooden water mill to make warm and friendly circumstance. Oppositely to the sub-gate, the main gate look sophisticated and harmonized with the surrounding environment. The sunburst design pavement pattern of the intersection looks like a direction sign that directs which way the cars should go.

The children's playground consistent of 'garden of sunset glow' and 'garden of morning' give the residents also a resting place in which they can relax looking at the sky. After passing through the driveway and going up on the top of slope, you can meet the garden of sunset glow, a small resting place, in which there are small sculptures and green plants. This place is like a station where people can stay to have rest passing by. The garden of morning shows the perfect harmony between the resting place and playground. Furthermore, you can see the children play in heartwarming mood from the wooden planter installed on the deck at the playground.

If you want to look all around this complex, what you have to know is only the point from which the walkway starts. After you enter in the walkway, you can meet the home-attached farms along the walkway linking every space and see the children play basketball on the basketball court. Furthermore, this walkway is not only a simple walkway on which you can simply go all around this complex but also a community center in which you can meet the others to share your love thanks to the cute places such as acupressure way and home-attached farms.

▲Tennis court

▲Resting place ▼Promenade

▲ Wood deck

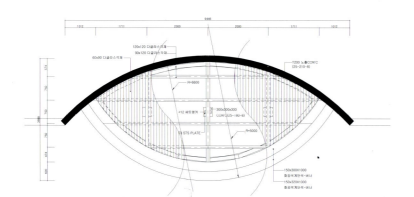

Game stage - plan

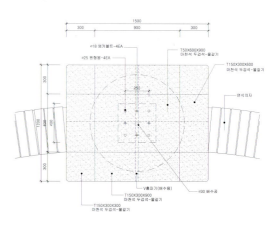

Serial bench - plan

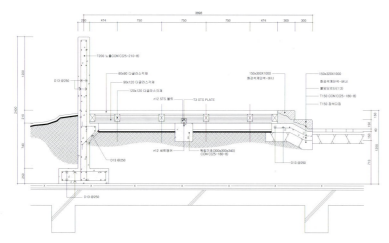

Game stage - Section

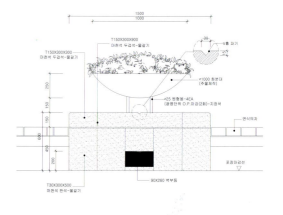

Planter bowl - elevation

▲Waterway

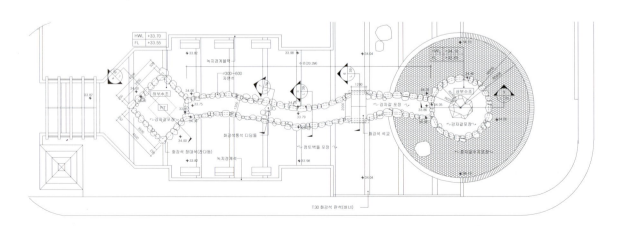

Part plan

▲Barefoot path

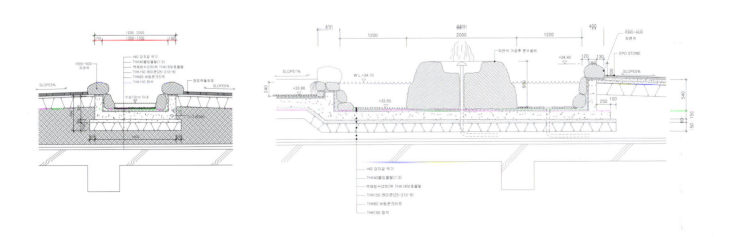

Water tank (upside)

Water tank (underside)

▲Playground

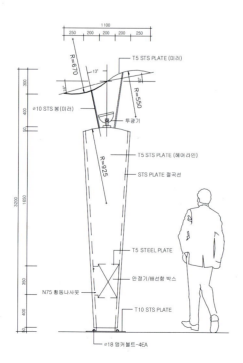

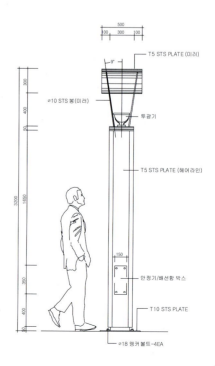

Lighting pillar - elevation

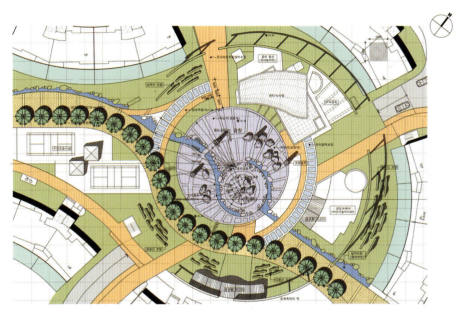

Landscape plan

▲Bird's eye view

▲View from center garden

조경설계 : (주)토문엔지니어링 건축사사무소
건축설계 : (주)토문엔지니어링 건축사사무소
대지위치 : 춘천시 우두동
지역지구 : 일반주거지역, 최고고도지구
용　　도 : 주거시설
대지면적 : 34,113.270㎡
건축면적 : 6,068.664㎡
연 면 적 : 66,103.099㎡
조경면적 : 8,628.90㎡
건 폐 율 : 17.78%
용 적 률 : 144.95%
규　　모 : 10~12층
외부마감 : 지붕 − THK 5 펀칭메탈

Landscape design : TOWMOON Engineering &
                   Architects Co., Ltd.
Architecture design : TOWMOON Engineering &
                      Architects Co., Ltd.
Area district ; Gerneral residential area, Height district
Function : Residential facility
Site area : 34,113.270㎡
Building area : 6,068.664㎡
Total floor area : 66,103.099㎡
Landscaped area : 8,628.90㎡
Building coverage ratio : 17.78%
Floor area ratio : 144.95%
Stories : 10~12FL
Ext. finish : Roof − THK 5 punching metal

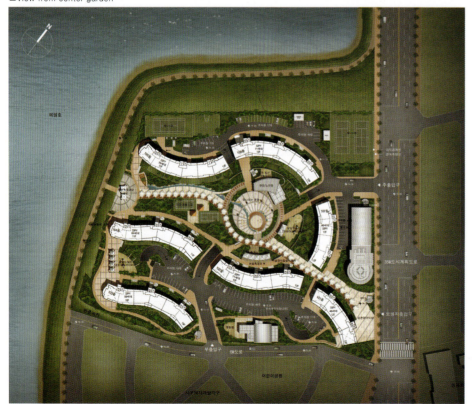

Landscape plan

▲View from building across the center gaden

▲View from road

▲View from center garden

▲Parking lot

대지는 2면이 의암호에 접해있는 사계절의 풍부한 자연 경관과 기존 도시의 Context를 고려, '자연·지역·인간친화' 적인 측면에서 쾌적하고 풍요로운 주거문화가 실현될 수 있도록 계획하였다.

자연환경요소의 단지 내 적극적 유입을 통해 호수의 풍경이 살아 숨쉬는 수변문화의 거리를 조성하여 축제의 마당으로 활용하고, 커뮤니티 공간의 다양화와 공공 공간의 활성화를 통해 공동체의 삶과 일상의 풍요로움을 담는 주거환경의 조성 및 기존 도시기능과 연계되어 호수의 정서를 반영한 유기적인 배치계획을 통해 상징적이고 기념적인 공간을 연출하고자 하였다. 주변경관과 연계되어 강촌 어귀마당, 중앙광장, 호반 축제마당으로 이어지는 주 보행축을 설정하여 자연과 도시를 잇는 오픈 스페이스를 계획하였으며, 차량동선은 중앙광장을 Under pass하도록 보차 동선을 분리했다.

한편, 보행동선은 차량접근이 일체 배제된 중앙광장을 중심으로 필로티 등을 통해 각 주동과 시설동을 연계하였으며 산책과 자전거 이용을 위해 단지외곽을 연결하는 일주도로를 설치하였다. 주거동의 형태는 호수(물결, 돛단배, 고동, 흐름, 흔적)의 이미지

화와 유기적인 배치를 통해 전세대에서의 의암호 조망이 가능하도록 하고, 호수 주변은 측세대를 계획하여 호수의 조망을 극대화 하여, 군인(直,强)의 반복되는 삶을 물결(曲,柔)속에서 일상의 여유로움을 되찾을 수 있게 하고자 하였다.

Since two sides of the site are adjacent to Uiam Lake, it realizes a comfortable and rich residential culture in the nature, district, human-friendly aspect considering the rich natural landscape of four seasons and context of existing city.

It establishes the street of waterside culture containing the vivid landscape of lake by attracting the natural elements into the complex actively in order to use it as a festival yard. By varying the community space and activating the public space, it creates the resident environment showing the living of community and rich daily life. It expresses a symbolic and memorable space by means of an organic arrangement plan reflecting the emotion of lake connecting with the function of existing city.

It plans an open space connecting nature with city by establishing the main walking axis connecting with the entrance plaza of riverside village, central plaza and festival yard of a lakeside in surrounding landscape. For the traffic circulation, it separates the traffic circulation from that of walking by making underpass the central plaza. The walking circulation connects each main building with facility building through pilotis centering on the central plaza in which all traffic approaches are excluded. It establishes a round road connecting with the complex outer block for walking and bicycle riding. The style of residence building is designed to view Uiam Lake from all households through making lake(wave, boat, whistle, stream, trace) as image and the organic arrangement. It plans to design side households for surroundings of the lake to maximize the view of lake so that the military man can enjoy a comfortable life in their monotonous life.

▲View of play garden

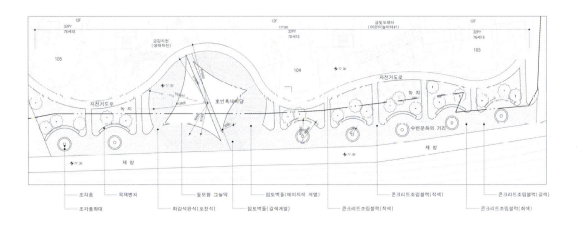

Water side floor plan

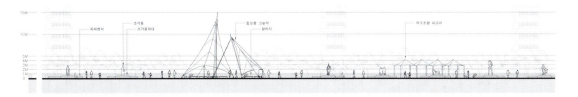

Water side elevation

Daelim e-Pyeonhan Sesang, Daebang-dong

▲Promenade

조 경 설 계 : 대림산업(주)+우리환경설계사무소
시　　공 : 대림산업(주) (02)2011-7114
위　　치 : 서울특별시 동작구 대방동 248-1번지
대 지 면 적 : 28,357㎡
조 경 면 적 : 8,821㎡
세 대 수 : 709세대

Landscape Design : Daelim Industrial Co., Ltd.+
　　　　　　　　　　Uri Environment Design Group
Construction : Daelim Industrial Co., Ltd.
Site Area : 28,357㎡
Landscape Area : 8,821㎡
Household : 709 Families

▲Landscape arts

'대방동 대림 e-편한세상(1차)' 은 푸르른 자연과 넓게 펼쳐진 체육 시설이 있는 곳이다.

이곳의 진입마당에는 소나무 수림대와 생태적 공법을 활용한 실개천을 조성하였고 주변으로 주민운동 시설이 설치되어 물의 소리를 들으며 사계절이 지나가는 단풍의 변화를 즐기며 운동을 할 수 있는 곳으로 계획되었다.

작은 폭포가 있는 어린이 놀이터와 이벤트 광장도 조성하여 주었으며 특히, 실개천의 경우 생태적인 공법의 조성으로 생물과 미생물간의 연결통로를 제공하면서 생태적인 연결고리 역할을 하도록 하였다.

'대방동 대림 e-편한세상(2차)' 은 단지가 작고 여유 공간이 부족하다 보니 1차 아파트와 달리 테마(thema)를 선정하는데 있어 많은 어려움이 있었다. 그러나 대림산업과 다임어소시에이츠와의 여러차례 미팅을 통하여 '야경' 이라는 테마와 방향을 설정하고 아파트 전체를 새로운 방식으로 접근하여 특화된 분위기를 연출하게 되었다.

특히, 차량이 통과하는 필로티의 경우 고급스러운 분위기에 석물과 초화류, 백자갈 등을 사용하여 화려하지만 고풍스러운 분위기를 보여주고 어둠이 내리는 시간이 되면 화려한 조명으로 피로티를 밝혀주도록 하였다. 단지 외부 옹벽에서도 조명 연출을 통하여 대방 2차아파트의 개념(concept)을 알릴 수 있도록 노력하였다.

Daelim 1st Condominium Complex, Daebang-dong, was built with green nature and widely spread athletic facilities. At the entrance ground, we made a pinewood and small stream by using ecological construction method. Around this ground, we built athletic facilities for local residents so that they could enjoy the athletic activity listening to the water streaming sound and seeing the leaves change their color. We also made an event square and children's playground in which a small waterfall was made. Especially, the small stream was made in the ecological method that provided an ecological connection path between lives and microorganisms.

Daelim 2nd Condominium Complex, Daebang-dong, was built in a small area without sufficient room provided for landscaping. In set of theme, we therefore, had a lot of other difficulties that we did not have in the 1st complex. We, however, could set the theme of night view and the landscaping direction through several meetings between Daerim Industry and Daim Associates and then we could approach the whole condominium complex in new way to produce a unique circumstance. Especially, the piloti through which cars pass by was designed to look flashy but classic using stone figures, flowers, white pebbles and etc under luxurious circumstance and to be lighted up by flashy lights when night coming. The retaining wall outside this complex was designed to light up in order to display the concept of 2nd condominium complex.

▲Landscape arts

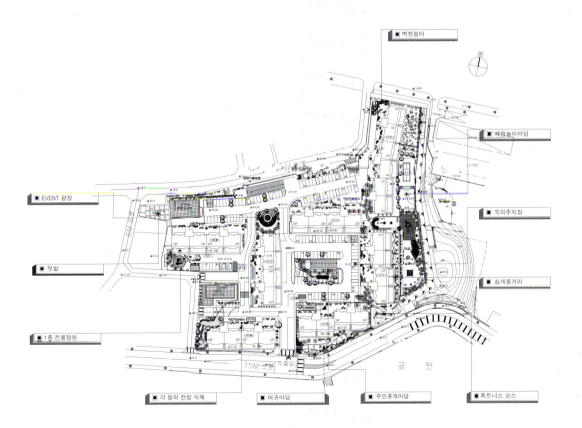

■ 벽천쉼터

■ EVENT 광장

■ 텃밭

■ 1층 전용정원

■ 각 동의 전정 식재   ■ 어귀마당   ■ 주민휴게마당   ■ 휘트니스 코스

■ 체험놀이마당

■ 옥외주차장

■ 실개울거리

Master plan

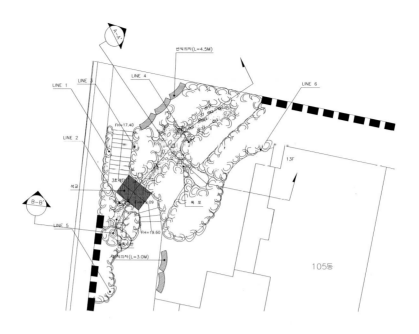

Planting plan

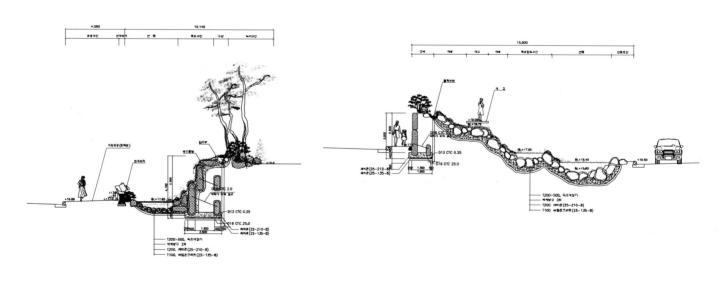

Section A-A'

Section B-B'

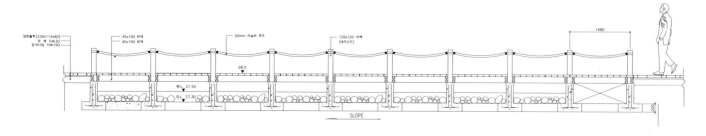

Section

▲Resting place

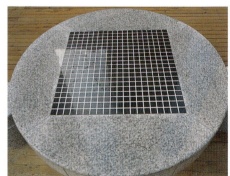

▲Paduk board

Plan & Construction

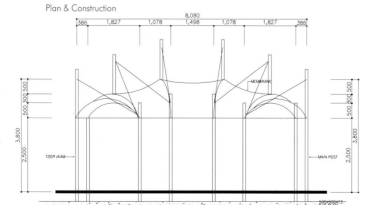

Front view

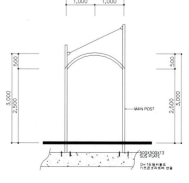

Side view

▲Event space

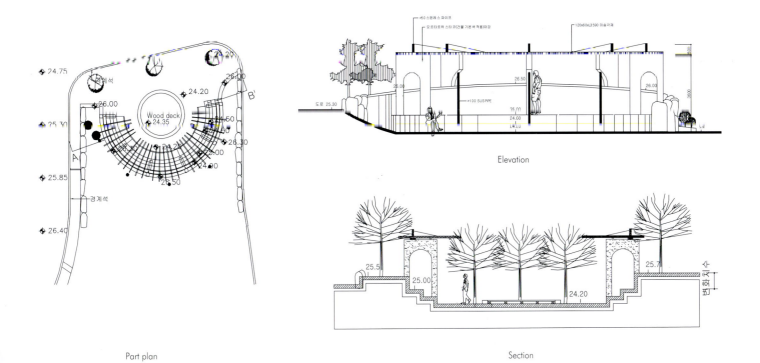

Part plan

Elevation

Section

▲Playground

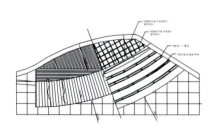

Part plan

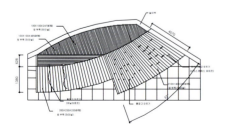

Part plan

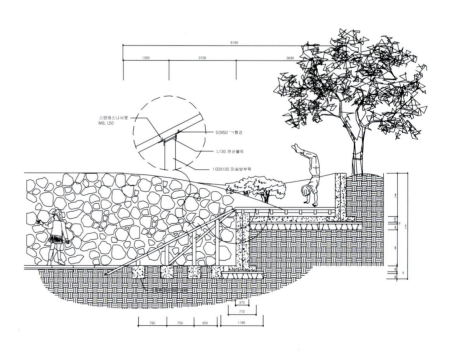

Elevation & detail

▲Wall fountain

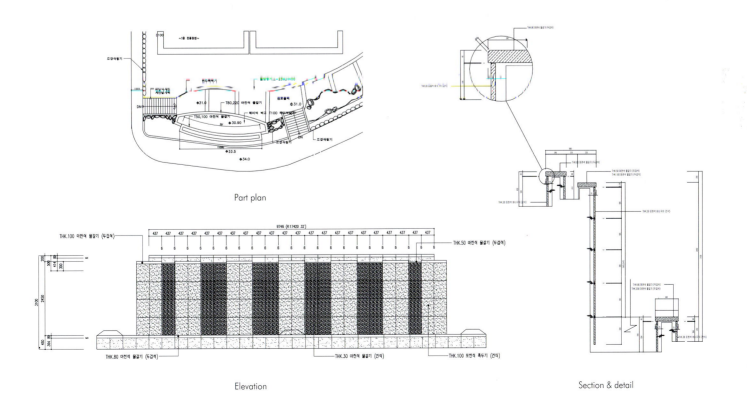

Part plan

Elevation

Section & detail

조경설계 : (주)우리엔 디자인펌 (02)572-3168
건축설계 : 삼하건축사사무소
조경시설 : 청우개발
조경식재 : (주)고운조경
위   치 : 서울시 구로구 신도림동 415-7번지
대지면적 : 5차 - 15,912.80㎡, 6차 - 4,361.00㎡
조경면적 : 5차 - 4,441.85㎡, 6차 - 895,96㎡
세 대 수 : 5차 - 362 세대, 6차 - 107 세대

Landscape Design : Uri Design Firm Co., Ltd.
Architecture Design : SAMHA Architects & Engineers
Landscape Facilities : Chung Woo Development
　　　　　　　　　　　　　Corporation
Landscape Planting : Gown Landscape Architecture
Site Area : 5-cha / 15,912.80㎡, 6-cha / 4,361.00㎡
Landscape Area : 5-cha / 4,441.85㎡, 6-cha / 895,96㎡
Household : 5-cha / 362 Families, 6-cha / 107 Families

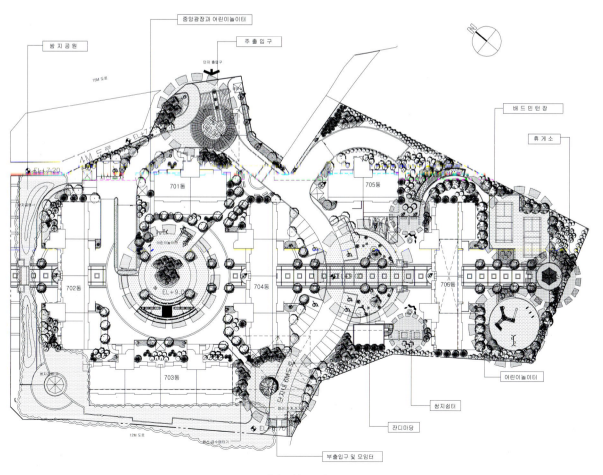

5-cha, Master plan

▲▼6-cha Environmental sculpture

신도림 5차 단지의 가장 큰 특징인 단지 중심을 가로지르는 보행축이 필로티를 통해 비스타(vista)를 이루며, 원형의 소광장들을 관통한다. 축의 양 끝은 보행자 출입구와 정자가 자리 잡고 있으며 왕벚나무가 식재되어 축을 강하게 살리는 구실을 하고 있다. 점토벽돌로 포상하여 아늑하고 따스한 분위기를 살리도록 계획하였다. 또한 원형식수대를 중심으로 어린이 놀이터와 바닥분수가 설치된 분수마당을 함께 조성하여 단지 중심의 동적인 활동의 지원성을 높임과 동시에, 조형적인 수목과 조각 소품들로 예술미를 강조한 원형잔디밭을 조성하여 정적인 휴게공간으로서의 지원성도 높였다.

신도림 6차 단지는 소규모 단지조경이므로 맞닿아 있는 공간들의 유기적 관계에 중점을 두어 두 동 사이에 위치한 원형광장과 휴게소, 어린이놀이터가 각각의 구실을 하면서 하나의 통일된 공간으로 보이도록 계획하였다.

중앙의 원형광장은 연잎에 앉은 개구리를 형상화한 개구리 분수에서 흘러내린 물이 계류를 이루며 안개 분수와 어우러져 경쾌한 경관을 연출하고, 어린이 놀이터의 가벽이 놀이가벽으로서의 역할 뿐 아니라 중앙광장을 둘러싸 광장의 배경이 되도록 하였다.

▲▼5-cha Environmental sculpture

The most distinctive feature is the axis for pedestrian, which is cutting across center of the block, penetrating pilotis to make Vista and leading to the small circular plazas. There are the entrances for the pedestrians and the pavilions at the end of the axis. Around there the big cherry trees are planted and these help adding the strong impression about the axis.

As this block has a widened paved area in total, the designers have planned it to make the atmosphere cozy by using the bricks. Around the circular bubbler the designers arranged the water fountain with children's park and deck fountain to support the villagers' activities and simultaneously they also displayed trees and sculptures for the landscape. Because of its small scale of Shindorim 6-Cha the importance had to be put in the organic relations between the spaces connected with. Therefore the designers would like to show that each of the facilities, for example the plaza, resting place and children's park, keeps its own function in harmony. These facilities are arranged between two blocks. A frog shaped water fountain streaming down water in the central plaza is harmonized with the fog water fountain. And the tentative wall for children's park plays the role of the background of the central plaza.

▲Playground

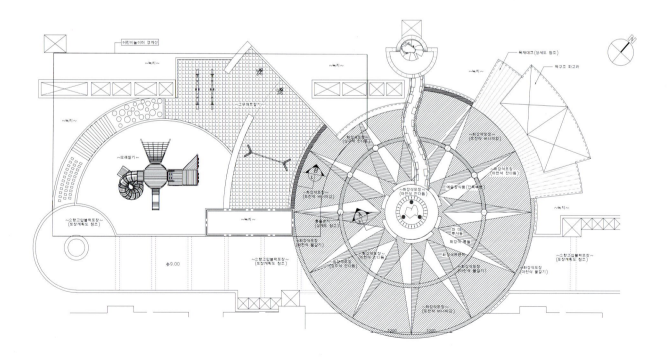

6-cha, Part plan (playground, central plaza, resting place)

▲Resting place

▲Barefoot path

Building

Jeju International Convention Center
Kyobo Tower
Geoje Culture Arts Center
Kitakyushu Environment Museum
Tseung Kwan O Community Center, Hong Kong
Mayfield Hotel
Hong Kong University of Science & Technology

▲Main night view

조 경 설 계 : 우정상 (경원대학교 교수)
건축계획설계 : 니혼 세케이
건축기본설계 : (주)천일건축
건축실시설계 : (주)종합건축사사무소 공간
대 지 위 치 : 제주도 서귀포시 중문동 2700
조 경 면 적 : 18,553.66㎡
대 지 면 적 : 54,876㎡
건 축 면 적 : 15,217.54㎡
연 면 적 : 62,125.10㎡
건 폐 율 : 27.73%
용 적 률 : 57.58%
규 모 : 지하2층, 지상 5층
주 차 대 수 : 359대
사 진 : 이중훈

Landscape design : Woo jeong sang (Kyunheon Univ. Professor)
Architecture design : Nihon Sekkei
Architecture Basic design : Cheonil Design & Architecture
Architecture execution : SPACE GROUP
Landscaped area : 18,553.66㎡
Site area : 54,876㎡
Building area : 15,217.54㎡
Total floor area : 62,125.10㎡
Building coverage ratio : 27.73%
Floor area ratio : 57.58%
Stories : B2, 5FL
Parking capacity : 359 cars
Photographer : Lee joong hoon

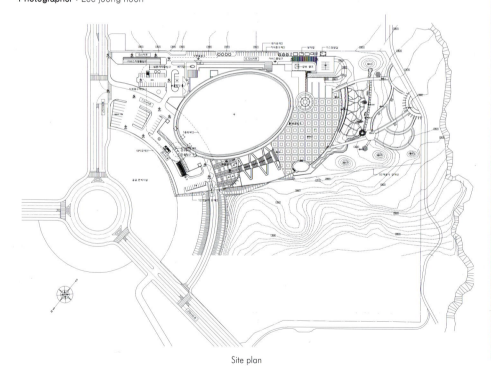

Site plan

▲Bird's eye view

■ Landscape construction by space

(1) 썬큰 가든 (Sunken Garden)
- 건물후면부의 후정으로 옥외활동 수용
- 벽천사용으로 광장의 생동감 부여
- 제주도의 이미지를 형상화한 계류 및 수조
- 포장은 점토벽돌로 하고 사이사이에 잔디를 식재하여 딱딱한 이미지를 완화토록 함
- Allows outdoor activities by a backyard in the rear of the building
- Gives out liveliness from a wall fountain in the square
- Mountain stream and a water tank representing an image of Jeju-do
- Softens a rigid image by clay brick pavement and lawn plantation in its gaps

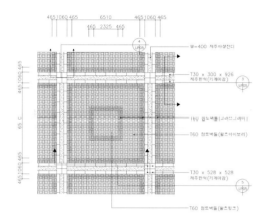

Sunken plaza -pavement A

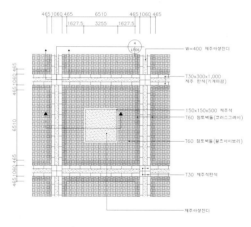

Sunken plaza -pavement B

(2) 계류 및 연못 (Mountain Stream and Pond)
- 담수조(-600)의 물을 계류형태로 낙하토록 하여 생동감 제공
- 계류사이 녹지부는 향토성이 짙은 소관목과 지피식재
- Provides vitality by water decent from a tank as a mountain stream
- Plantation of bushes and ground covers of strong locality in the green areas between mountain streams

(3) 야생화 초지 (Wild Flower Field)
- 보행데크를 따라 관찰 및 사진촬영장소 제공
- 조각의 배치로 문화공간 제공
- 해안산책로와 보행동선과 연계한 공개공지
- Provides space for observation and photo along walking decks

- Offers a cultural space by the arrangement of sculptures
- Public space that connects coastline walk with walking line

(4) 벽천 (Wall Fountain)
- 계류와 선큰광장의 연결부위로 계류로부터 물을 받아 상부 연못(B)에서 하부 연못(C)사이에 벽천을 두어 물이 낙하토록하여 물의 생동감 및 청량감을 불어 넣어 컨벤션센터의 역동적 이미지를 향상시킴
- Emphasizes vigorous image of the convention center by installing a wall fountain between the upper pond(B) and the lower pond(C), where water falls in from the connection of mountain stream and sunken garden, bringing a refreshing, lively feel

(5) 후면부 광장 (Rear Courtyard)
- 동산과 공개공지가 함께 이루는 공간으로 제주의 상징인 한라산을 형상화한 조형물과 각종 식물이 어우러져 건물과 균형을 이루고 또 해안산책로와 건물의 보행 중심 동선이 연계된 공간으로 타원형의 컨벤션센터 이미지가 가장 조화가 이루어지는 공간
A space made of a garden and public space. Landscape arts, which represents Hallasan(Mt.), the symbol of Jeju-do, and various kinds of plants are joined together to be in harmony with the building. Connection area of coastline walk and walk-centered traffic line creates harmony with the image of oval convention center.

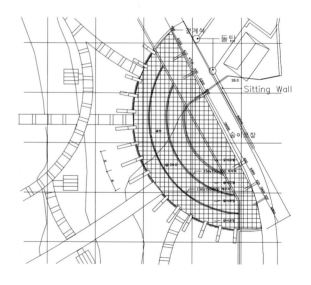

Rear courtyard

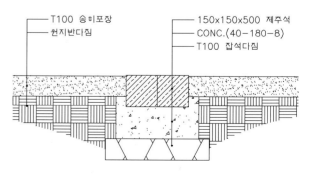

Pavement section

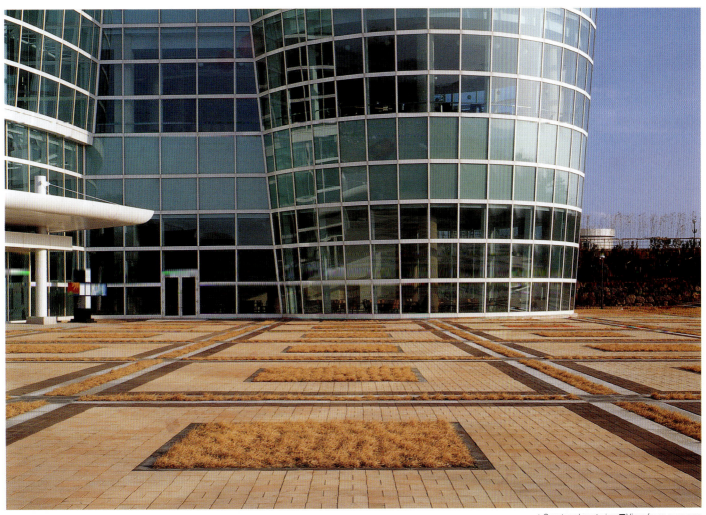

▲Courtyard part view▼View from over sea

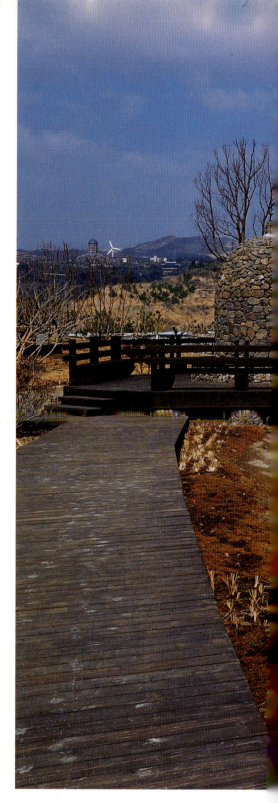

▲ Embrnkment with curious rock

컨벤션센터는 상업회의와 학술회의, 여러 이벤트와 집회를 위한 하나의 건물에 지나지 않는다. 그러나 국제컨벤션센터가 지역의 경제에 미치는 파급효과는 매우 커서 그 지역 산업활동의 중심이 되고, 교통, 서비스, 관광산업 등과 연계됨으로써 경제 활성화에 구심점 역할을 한다.

이에 현재 우리나라의 여러 지방자치단체가 컨벤션센터에 관심을 가지고 건립 구상을 검토하거나 진행 중에 있다.

제주국제컨벤션센타(Jeju International Convention Center, 이하 CICC)의 건립은 1996년 여름, 제주도의 도 승격 50주년 기념행사에서 제주도에 컨벤션센터의 필요성이 제안된 일년 뒤 (주)제주국

제컨벤션센터가 창립되면서 시작되었다. 이는 그 동안 제주에서 각종 정상회담, 외무회담, 총리회담 등이 있었고, 제주가 국제 외교의 창구 역할을 해왔음을 볼 때 뒤늦은 감마저 없지 않다. 1997년 가을, 기본계획에 대한 디자인 공모전이 열렸고, SOM, Nihon Sekkei등 세계 여러 업체들이 참가한 가운데 Nihon Sekkei의 안이 선정되어 (주)천일건축이 기본설계를 맡았다. 당시 기본설계안은 회의실 규모 5,000석의 컨벤션센터에 호텔, 아이맥스관, 쇼핑센타 등 별동의 건물들을 함께 건립하는 단지 계획이었으나 이후 회의실 규모가 3,500석인 컨벤션센터만 우선적으로 설계하도록 그 규모가 축소되었다. 1999년 10월에 있은 실시설계 및 공사에 대한 턴키

발주에는 호텔을 CICC와 함께 지을 것과 CICC에 투자할 것을 요구하는 조건이 붙었으며, 총 다섯 팀 중 (주)대우건설 + (주)공간종합건축사사무소가 이에 응하여 선정되었다. (주)공간건축은 수정된 조건 아래 Nihon Sekkei의 기본계획을 바탕으로 설계에 착수, 계획설계 및 실시설계를 하였으며, 현재 CICC 부분의 토공사가 진행 중에 있다. 2002년 12월에 완공하여 2003년 1월, 오픈할 계획이다.

CICC는 중문관광단지 인근의 중문 2단계 동부 지구에 속해 있고, 여미지식물원, 주상절리, 천지연폭포 등의 관광 명소들을 잇는 선상에 위치하여 중문 2단계 관광단지의 첫 사업으로서, 또 관광지의 중간 연결지로서 중요성을 가진다.

▲Around landscape

CICC로의 진입동선은 나선에서 따온 곡선으로 관광객을 자연스럽게 지하 2층 선큰광장으로 유도하여, VIP 동선, 직원 동선 및 서비스 동선을 별도로 마련하였다. CICC의 특징적 이미지는 타원형의 매스이다. 이는 섬의 모양에서 유추한 것으로 장축은 한라산의 정상을 향하며 동시에 태평양을 지향한다. 또 커튼월의 투명 유리는 바다가 측에 사용하여 외부자연이 관입, 관류되도록 하였다. 타원형 매스에는 작은 원형 매스가 이어져 전체 건물에 리듬감을 부여하고, 동측면의 사각 불투명 매스는 사무실, 소회의실 등의 기능을 담당하며 균형감을 준다.

컨벤션센터의 특성상 내부에는 큰 행사시 사용하는 대형공간이 요구됨과 동시에 이 대형공간들이 평상

시에도 활용 가능해야 한다.

그래서 전시실, 연회실, 회의실 등에 이동식 칸막이를 설치하여 대형 및 소형 행사에 모두 대처 가능토록 하였다. 특히 3,500석의 회의실은 1,500석이 고정식 좌석에 바닥이 경사져 있고, 2,000석은 이동식 좌석으로 평바닥이어서 2개 실로 구획하면 각기 다른 용도의 특징적 공간이 된다.

컨벤션센터는 교통 접근성이 우수한 도심에 입지하기도 하지만(현재 삼성동에 건립된 ASEM이 여기에 속한다) 관광거점지역에 들어선 경우(Hawaii Convention Center, Mytle Bead Convention Center 등이 있다) 리조트를 겸할 수 있는 장점으로 최근 크게 활성화되는 추세이다.

CICC는 제주의 '삼보, 삼려'라고 손꼽히는 천혜의 자연환경과 인심, 맛난 음식에 힘입어 각종 대규모 국제 행사들을 유치하기에 크게 유리할 것으로 생각된다. 가깝게는 일산 등 앞으로 계획될 우리나라 각자의 컨벤션센타의 발전적 방향을 제시해 주고, 멀게는 2003년 오픈 이후 국제적 컨벤션센터로 역할하여, 외교와 관광산업에 기여하기를 기대해본다.

〈글 / (주)종합건축사사무소 공간〉

A convention center is just a building for commercial conferences, academic conferences, various events and meetings. However since the Jeju International Convention Center enormously exerts

influence on the local economy, it becomes the center of local industry activities and plays a central role to activate economy connected with traffic, service, and tourist industry. Therefore various municipal bodies in Korea review or plan to establish a convention center. The plan for the establishment of Jeju International Convention Center (hereinafter CICC) was followed by the foundation of Jeju International Convention Center Company one year after that a convention center in Jeju is suggested to be necessary in the summer 1996 on the 50th anniversary of Jeju province. It is a little bit belated to plan a convention center in Jeju considering that there have been various summit meetings, diplomatic meetings, and premier meetings in Jeju to play a

role of window for the international diplomacy. In the autumn 1997, a competition for design concept was held, in which international companies such as SOM and Nihon Sekkei participated. The planning of Nihon Sekkei was selected and Cheonil Architecture was assigned for the design development. The original design development was to establish annexes such as hotel, I Max hall, and shopping center together with the convention center of 5,000 - seat meeting room. However the plan was reduced to construct the convention center of 3,500 - seat meeting room first. The turnkey ordering for implementation design and construction in October 1999 was conditioned to construct a hotel with CICC and invest in CICC. Out of five candidates,

Daewoo Engineering & Construction + Space Group were selected. Space Group started to design based on the basic planning of Nihon Sekkei under the changed conditions in order to conduct the schematic design and implementation design. Space Group is now conducting public works for the part of CICC. It is expected to complete the construction in December 2002 and open in January 2003. CICC belongs to the eastern zone of Jungmun Complex 2 neighbouring to Jungmun Tourism Complex and is located in the line of tourist places such as Yeomiji Botanic Garden, pillar-shaped joint, and Cheonjiyeon Waterfall, which furnishes an important meaning as the first project of the tourist Jungmun Complex 2 and an intermediate connect-

▲Courtyard part view

ing place of the tourist sites. The entrance traffic line toward CICC is a curve modeled from a spiral to lead the tourists to the sunken plaza on the underground second floor, which is separated from the traffic lines for VIP, employees and service. The most characteristic image of CICC comes from the oval mass, which is modeled from the shape of island. The long axis faces toward the summit of Mt. Halla and the Pacific at the same time. In addition, the transparent glass of curtain wall is designed with the image of sea to introduce the exterior natural environment into the inside. The oval mass consisting of small circular masses distributes rhythm to the whole building, and the rectangular opaque mass functions as offices and small meeting rooms and

gives balance. Considering the characteristics of a convention center, a large-sized space is required to hold huge events and this large-sized space should be used at normal times. It installs movable partitions for the exhibition room, banquet room and meeting room to cope with the small- and large-sized events. In particular, the meeting room of 3,500 seats consists of two spaces; one is for 1,500 fixed seats on the inclined floor and the other is for 2,000 movable seats on the flat floor, which can be separated to use for various purposes by dividing it into two rooms. While some convention centers are located in the downtown with an excellent traffic approach (e.g. ASEM in Samsung-dong), a convention center in a tourist basis is recently getting popu-

lar because of advantages of a convention center with a resort function (e.g. Hawaii Convention Center, Mytle Bead Convention Center). CICC has advantageous terms to attract various large-sized international events owing to the beautiful natural environment, good-hearted people, and delicious food of Jeju. This project would suggest a developmental direction for the convention center in Korea including a convention center to be constructed in Ilsan. We expect that CICC would contribute to the diplomacy and tourist industry with its great role of an international convention center after opening in 2003.

(written by SPACE GROUP)

▲Paved road with stone

▲Formative art work

▲View of parking lot

▲Formative art work

▲Steet lamp

건축기본설계 : 마리오 보타
건축실시설계 : (주)창조종합건축사사무소
대지위치 : 서초구 서초동 1303
지역지구 : 일반상업지역, 1종미관지구, 2종미관지구
조경면적 : 2,155m
대지면적 : 6,770.20㎡
건축면적 : 3,042.38㎡
연 면 적 : 92,797.52㎡
건 폐 율 : 44.94%
용 적 률 : 796.60%
규 모 : 지하8층, 지상25층
구 조 : 지상 - 철골조, 철근콘크리트조
         지하 - 철골철근콘크리트조
외부마감 : PC패널, 벽돌마감

Architecture basic design : Mario Botta
Execution design : Changjo Architect, Inc.
Area district : General commercial area,
                First rate fine sight district,
                Secoud class fine view district
Landscaped area : 2,155m
Site area : 6,770.20㎡
Building area : 3,042.38㎡
Total floor area : 92,797.52㎡
Building coverage ratio : 44.94%
Floor area ratio : 796.60%
Stories : 8B, 25FL
Structure : Ground — Steel, Reinforced concrete
            Underground —
            Steel framed reinforced concrete
Ext. finish : PC panel, Brick

▲View from building across the road

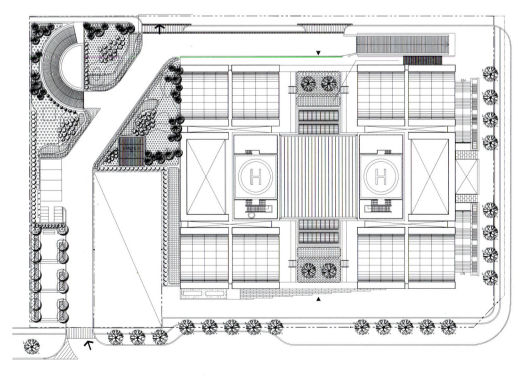

Site plan

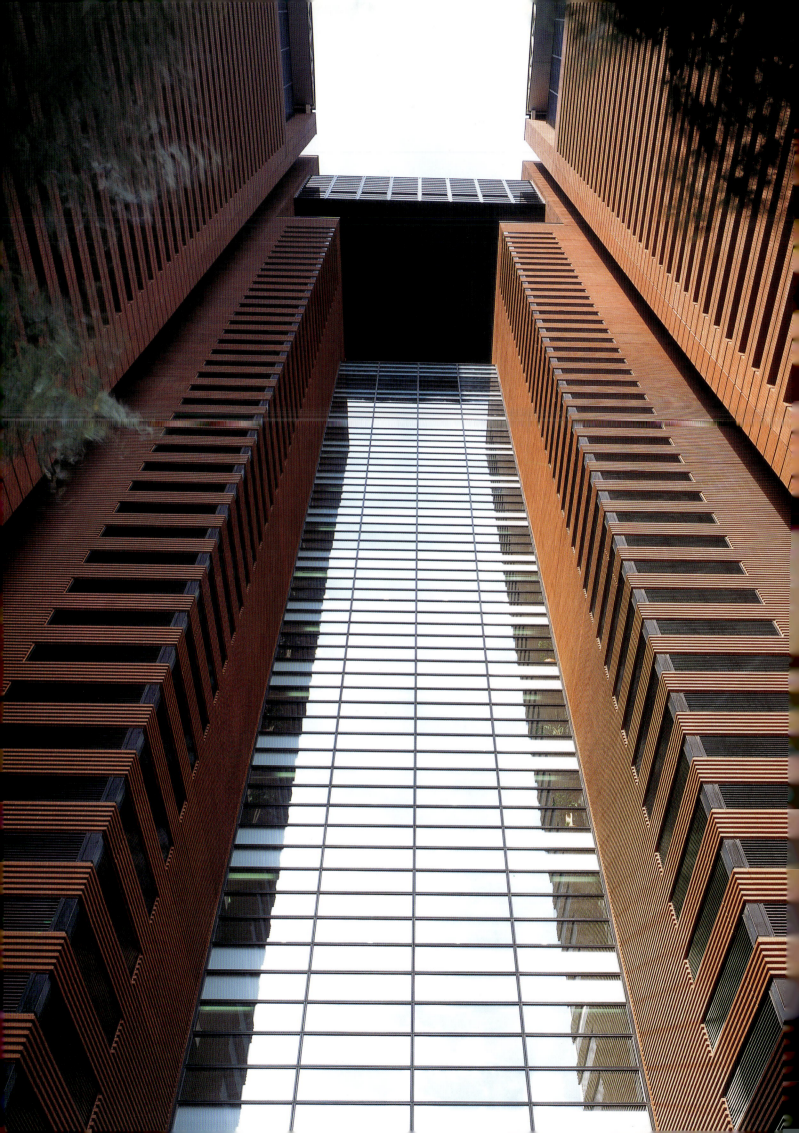

■ Planting Construction

· 상록교목류: 조형소나무 외 3종 122주
· 낙엽교목류: 느티나무외 2종 85주
· 관목류: 연산홍 포함 4,680주
· 초화류: 수호초, 담쟁이외 24,761주
· 계 : 29,441주

Pine

Crape myrtle

Zelkova

Rhododendron indicum

Yew

Pinus parviflora

▲Enterence view

▲View from Gangam Road

▲Open site between the twin tower

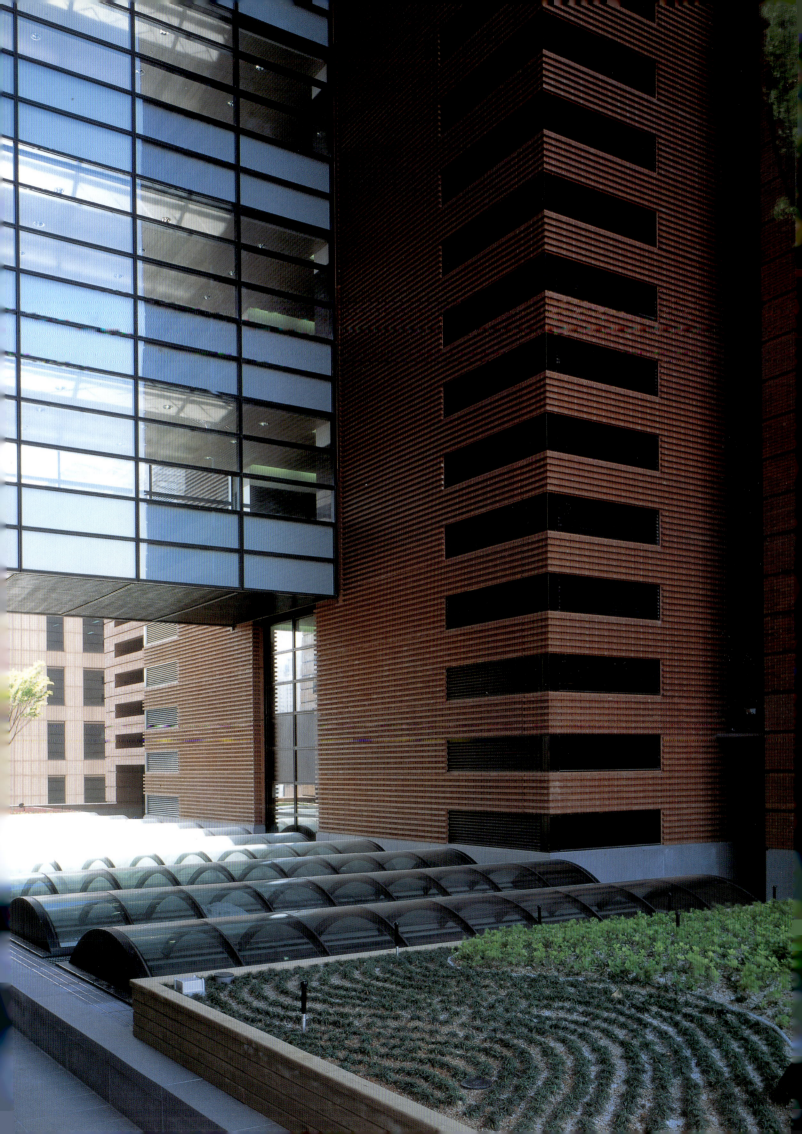

교보강남타워는 서울의 새 중심인 강남대로와 사평로가 교차하는 곳에 위치해있다. 본 건물은 주변의 스틸과 유리로 이루어진 개방적인 다른 건물들과는 확연하게 다르게 매시브하고 폐쇄적인 모습을 하고 있다. 이러한 중세의 거대한 요새 같은 이미지의 타워 형상은 현대적인 도시 건물들에 익숙해져 있는 사람들에게 그들의 방향을 확인할 수 있는 새로운 이정표 역할을 할 것이다.

2개의 쌍둥이 타워는 3개 층으로 이루어진 하단부 매스 위에 세워져 있다. 2개의 쌍둥이 타워 사이에 설치된 18m 폭의 천창은 하단부 매스 속에 이루어지는 인테리어 공간을 자연광으로 비출수 있도록 한다. 각각의 타워는 수직의 3개 볼륨으로 이루어 지고 있으며, 연속된 창문들은 수직적 느낌이 강조된 외관에 수평적인 작은 선들을 그려줌으로서 전적으로 수직, 수평의 발란스를 이루어준다. 쌍둥이 타워를 연결하는 공중 브릿지는 각 독립된 타워간의 원활한 동선을 만들어준다. 또한 23층에 위치한 또 하나의 거대한 브릿지는 2개의 녹립된 타워를 묶어수면서, 스페셜 이벤트 등 다양한 행사의 장소로도 사용될 수 있다.

외부공간

빌딩 바로 앞에 펼쳐지는 조경공간은 도시적 활동의 연장된 공간으로서 계획되었다. 특히 2개의 주요 도로가 교차하는 장소로서 그 역할은 더더욱 중요하다. 이러한 2개의 도로와 나란한 동측과 북측의 공간은 보행자들에게 편리하도록 설계하였다. 조경공간은 남측에 공개공지에 이웃하여 집중적 배치되어 있으며, 차량의 지하주차장 진출입은 서측에 위치하여 있다.

내부공간

고층빌딩의 내부공간은 외부형태가 좌우한다. 본 건물은 쌍둥이타워로 디자인 되었기 때문에 수직동선 및 각종 설비를 담당할 중요한 코아가 양 타워에 위치하게 되었다.

저층부

저층부는 중앙의 메인로비를 중심으로 하여 3개 층으로 이루어졌다. 메인 로비는 건물의 정중앙에 위치하고 있으며 저층부 지붕층에 설치된 천창을 통하여 유입된 자연광이 3개의 각층에 모두 전달될 수 있도록 중정식으로 이루어져 있다. 3개 층에 걸쳐 보이드 되어 있는 메인로비는 방문자들에게 한눈에 건물 내부의 방향을 감지할 수 있도록 하여준다. 1층에는 은행과 보험회사가 위치해 있으며, 2, 3층에는 업무시설이 입주할 예정이다.

쌍둥이타워

2개의 타워는 업무전용의 공간이다. 건물형태에 의하여 방문자는 내부공간을 쉽게 이해할 수 있다. 각층의 바다 전체는 대형 유리 창문과 직사광선을 피할 수 있도록 설계된 고정형 차양을 통하여 유입된 자연광에 의하여 골고루 비춰진다. 각층마다의 색다른 요구에 내부공간은 손쉽게 적응될 수 있는 유연한 구성으로 되어있다. 각층은 개방적 혹은 폐쇄적 칸막이 구조 등이 자유롭게 설치될 수 있다. 이와 함께 IBS(지능형 건물 시스템)는 최상의 근무환경을 제공한다. 각 2개의 층마다 독립된 2개의 공간의 코아를 연결하는 작은 브릿지가 있다.

23층

23층, 2개의 타워 사이에 위치한 스페셜 이벤트 룸은 서울 동서방향의 자유로운 경관을 제공한다. 이 다목적 공간은 철골과 유리를 사용하여 최대의 개방감을 주면서 동시에 양측에 위치한 업무공간을 연결하는 브릿지 역할도 함께 수행한다.

Kyobo Gangnam Tower is located where Sapyeongro crosses Gangnam Road, the new center of Seoul. This building gives a massive and closed atmosphere differently from other open buildings consisted of steel and glass in surroundings. The shape of tower with the image of a huge fortress in the middle ages would play a role of a new milestone to identify the direction for the people who are accustomed to the urban buildings.

Two twin towers are established on the lower mass consisting of three floors. The ceiling of 18m wide established between two twin towers lights the interior space in the lower mass with the natural light. Each tower consists of three vertical volumes and the consecutive windows make the horizontal and vertical balance by drawing the small horizontal lines in the appearance emphasized with the vertical feeling. The air bridge connecting with the twin tower makes the smooth traffic line between each independent tower. In addition, the huge bridge on the 23rd floor combines two independent towers to be used as a place for various events such as special events.

External Space

The landscape space in front of the building is planned as an extended space for the urban activities.

Moreover, its role is very important as a place where two main roads are crossing. The space in the east and north in parallel with these two roads are designed to give comfort to the passengers. The landscape space is intensively arranged adjacent to the open site in the south and the entrance and exit for the underground parking lot is located in the west.

Internal Space

The internal space in a high-rise building depends on the external appearance. Since this building is designed as a twin tower, the important core in charge for the vertical traffic line and various facilities is located in both tower.

Lower Part

The lower part is consisted of three floors centering on the main lobby in the center. The main lobby is located in the very center of the building as a courtyard style so that the natural light attracted through the skylight in the roof floor of the lower part can be transferred to each three floor. The main lobby voided cross three floors makes it possible for visitors to sense the direction of the inside of building at a look. On the first floor, a bank and insurance company are situated and office facilities are scheduled to situate on the second and third floor.

Twin Tower

Two towers are a space for office only. The visitors can understand the internal space easily by means of the building style. The whole floor of each floor is lighted by the natural light equally through the large-sized glass window and the fixed blind designed so as to avoid a direct ray of light. The inside space is flexibly constituted so as to be adapted to the different demands of each floor. The partition structure of open or close style can be freely established on each floor. In addition, IBS(Intelligent Building System) offers the best working environment. There is a small bridge connecting two independent spaces on each floor.

23rd floor

The special event room located between two towers on the 23rd floor offers a free landscape to the east and west in Seoul. This multiple space gives an open feeling to the utmost using steel and glass and plays a role of bridge connecting the office space located on both.

▲Vacant lot for the public

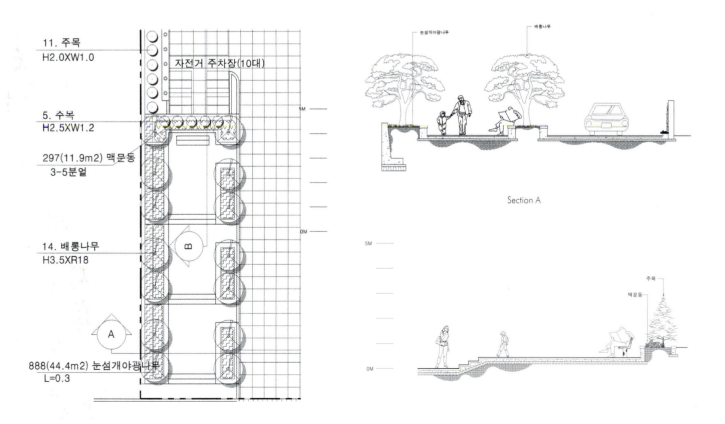

11. 주목
H2.0XW1.0

자전거 주차장(10대)

5. 수복
H2.5XW1.2

297(11.9m2) 맥문동
3-5분얼

14. 배롱나무
H3.5XR18

888(44.4m2) 눈섬개야광나무
L=0.3

눈섬개야광나무   배롱나무

Section A

주목

맥문동

Site plan of vacant lot for the public

Section B

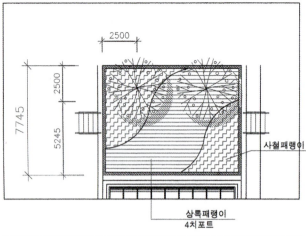

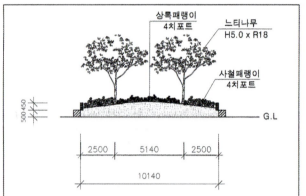

Roof landscape architecture plan from westside

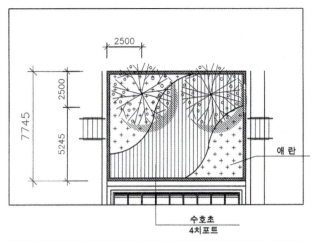

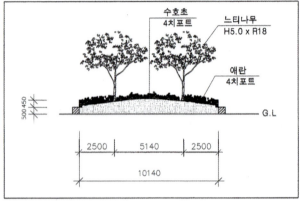

Roof landscape architecture plan from Gangnam Road

▲Air bridge between the twin tower

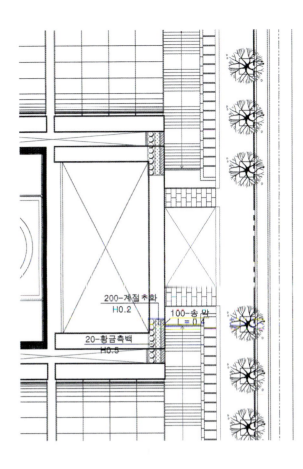

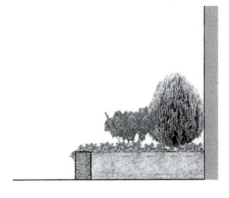

Sunken section

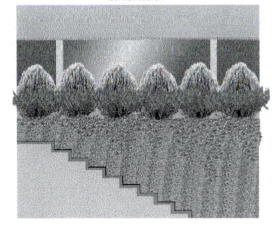

Roof landscape architecture plan from Gangnam RoadSite plan of sunken

Sunken elevation

▲View of stair stream near sunken

Night view of stair stream near sunken ▼ Night view of front side

Geoje Culture Arts Center

조경설계 : 오브제플랜
건축설계 : (주)아도무 종합건축사사무소
시   공 : (주)한진중공업
대지위치 : 거제시 장승포동 426-33
지역지구 : 일반상업지역. 일반주거지역
대지면적 : 25,749㎡
건축면적 : 10,691.99㎡
연 면 적 : 20,243.60㎡
건 폐 율 : 41.52%
용 적 률 : 60.54%
규   모 : 본관동-지하2층, 지상3층
           별관동-지하1층, 지상 4층
주차대수 : 175대
외부마감 : 화강석버너구이, 스테인리스 스틸 플레이트
사   진 : 채수옥

Landscape design : Objet plan
Architecture design : a-dome Architects & Engineers Inc.
Construction : Hanjin Heavy industries & Construction Co.,Ltd.
Area district : General commercial area, General residential area
Site area : 25,749㎡
Building area : 10,691.99㎡
Total floor area : 20,243.60㎡
Building coverage ratio : 41.52%
Floor area ratio : 60.54%
Stories : Main building-B2, 3FL
          Annex-B1, 4FL
Structure : Reinforced concrete, Steel
Parking capacity : 175 cars
Ext. finish : Granite flamed, Stainless steel plate
Photographer : Chae su ok

Site plan

▲View over the sea

거제도 남단의 천혜의 항구인 장승포항에 따뜻하고
소박하여 의미있는 새로운 조형물로써 찾는 이들의
가슴속에 하나하나의 등불이고 싶다.
거제는 조선공업의 메카이자 풍부한 문화유산과 아
름다운 자연경관을 간직한 채 자연과 인간이 함께
살아가는 천혜의 땅이다. 세계굴지의 조선공단이 주
는 지역적 아이덴티니(Identity)를 부각시킬 수 있
는 건축적 모티프(Motif)를 현대적 감각으로 재해석
하여 산과 바다가 어우러진 자연과 함께 할 수 있는
문화예술의 장을 마련코자 한다.
외부로 최대한의 조망을 확보하기 위한 방사형 배치
는 본관과 별관의 매스를 이어주는 데크와 더불어
다양한 변화를 갖는 정면성을 갖는다. 경사인 지
형적 환경을 이용한 볼륨의 점층적 상승은 단계적인
시각적 변화를 유도하며 데크에 의한 기단형식으로
안정감을 더한다. 2단구성으로 된 데크는 협소한 대
지에서 바다를 향한 오픈 스페이스의 확보 및 두 진
입동선의 연결점이기도하다. 기단(Deck)이 갖는 강
한 수평적 요소 속에서 열주량의 수직적 요소는 스

며드는 빛의 변화속에서 다양한 표정을 연출한다.
장승포항으로 유입되는 조망을 고려한 정면성의 부
여는 돛의 이미지를 조형화한 날개의 반복적 사용으
로 변화하고 발전하는 지역의 이미지를 구현한다.
외부의 풍부한 개방감에 반해 내부의 절제된 공간은
빛의 변화에 의한 극적공간의 체험을 유도한다. 리
듬감 있는 로비의 벽은 무대에서의 감흥을 여운으로
간직하게 해주며 필로티를 통한 외부로의 연계는 펼
쳐진 바다와 더불어 절정을 이루게 한다.
본 계획은 문화예술 공연기능과 스포츠레져 및 리조
트 시설을 연계한 복합 문화공간으로 시민들의 다양
한 휴식과 활력을 주며 21C 관광 거제를 선도하게
될 것이다.

It is a new formative sculpture of a warm and simple
meaning for Jangseungpo Port, the gift of nature in
the southern of Geoje Island to be a bright lamp for
every visitor.

Geoje is the Mecca of shipbuilding industry and the
land of gift of nature where human being lives
together with nature keeping with its rich cultural
inheritances and beautiful landscape. We intended to
construct a cultural and art field to attract the nature
with mountains and sea by reinterpreting the
architectural motif as a modern sense in order to
emphasize the local identity of shipbuilding
complex of international level. The arrangement of a
radial shape secures the frontality with various
changes together with deck that is connecting with
the mass of headquarters and outbuilding in order to
secure the maximum view toward outside. The
gradual ascent of volume using the geographical
environment of slope induces the gradual visual
changes, and the deck provides with stability by
means of deck. The deck consisting of two
platforms is the connecting point of two entrance
circulations for securing the open space toward the

▲Bird's eye view

sea from the narrow site. The vertical elements of
colonnadein the strong horizontal elements of deck
produce various expressions in the change of light.
To distribute the frontality considering the view
introduced to Jangseungpo Port incorporates the
image of district that is changing and developing by
using the image of sail as a formative wing
repeatedly.

The temperate space of inside attracts the experience
of dramatic space by means of changes of the light
differently from the rich open feeling of outside. The
rhythmical wall of lobby keeps the excitement of
stage as an after taste and the connection toward
outside through pilotis makes the climax together
with the sea. This plan will lead the tourist Geoje
Island for the 21st century by providing citizens with
various relaxation and energy as a complex culture
space connected with culture, art and performance
function, sports leisure and resorts facilities.

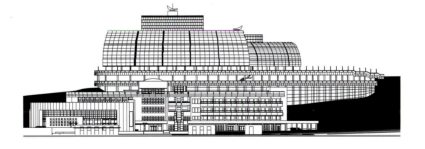

Front elevation

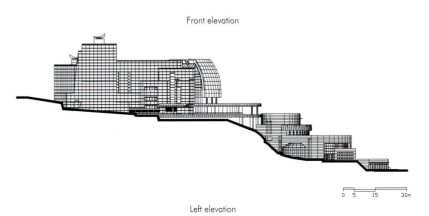

0 5 15 30m

Left elevation

▲View from street

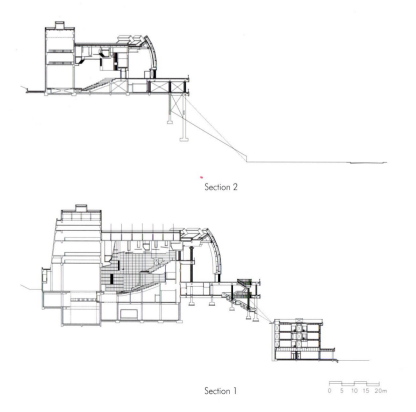

Section 2

Section 1

0 5 10 15 20m

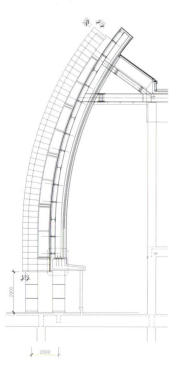

Section 3

Kitakyushu Environment Museum

위　치 : 후쿠오카 키타큐슈시
대지면적 : 4,100㎡
건축면적 : 1,596㎡
연면적 : 2,061㎡
규　모 : 지상 2층
구　조 : 철근콘크리트조, 철골조
사　진 : 요시하루 마츠무라

Location : Kitakyushu-shi, Fukuoka
Site area : 4,100㎡
Building area : 1,596㎡
Total floor area : 2,061㎡
Stories : 2FL
Structure : Reinforced concrete, Steel frame
Photographer : Yosiharu Matsumura

키타큐슈 환경 박물관의 주제는 환경이다. 무공해와 에너지 절약이 공사 도중과 완공 후에 요구되며, 이는 건물 설계에서도 마찬가지이다. 이 건물은 세 가지 기능을 갖는다. '전시', '시각적 외양', '행정 사무실'이 그것이다. 이 건물은 또한 세 가지 재료를 사용하여 건축되었다. '철강', '콘크리트' 그리고 '목재' (건설용, 벽, 나무 식재)이다. 건물 형태는 또한 세 가지 형태를 갖는다. 두 개의 사각 형태와 한 개의 구형이다. 자연적 재료들은 가능한 많이 사용되고 건물 이용의 융통성이 장래를 위해 고려된다.

광전지 발생과 풍력 발생이 에너지의 효과적인 활용을 위해 도입되었다. 벽 표면과 옥상을 녹지화하고 창문 지붕을 이용해 실내 온도와 실외 온도사이의 열전도를 줄인다. 녹지는 상쾌한 기분을 주고 열섬 효과를 감소시킨다.

Environment is the theme of Kitakyushu Environment Museum. Zero emissions and energy conservation are required during and after the construction, and also for the building design. The building has three functions: 'exhibition', 'visual presentation' and 'administrative offices'. The building was also constructed with three materials: 'steel', 'concrete', and 'wood' (for construction, walls, and tree planting). The building shape also has three forms : two squares and one sphere. Natural materials were used as much as possible and flexibility in building usage was considered for the future.

Photovoltaic generation and wind power generation were introduced for effective utilization of energy. Greening the wall surface and rooftop and reducing heat transfer between room temperature and outside temperature by window roofs were also introduced. Greens give pleasant feelings and reduce the heat island effect.

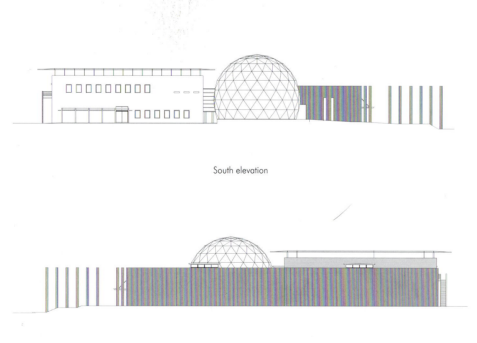

South elevation

North elevation

▲View form garden

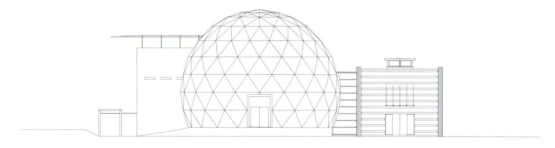

East elevation

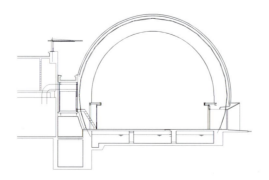

South section

▲Enterence view

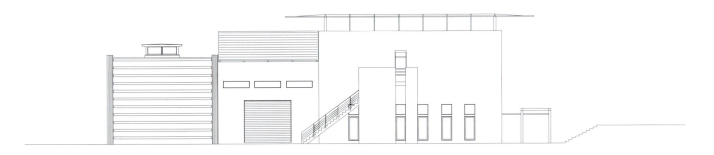

West elevation

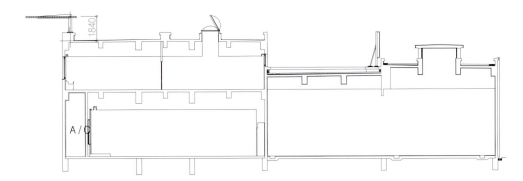

East section

1. Entrance
2. Exhibition hall
3. Audio-visual hall
4. Conference hall
5. Office
6. Director room
7. Mechanical
8. Lobby
9. Lecturer room
10. Environment practice room
11. Conference room
12. Storage

▲Exhibition hall

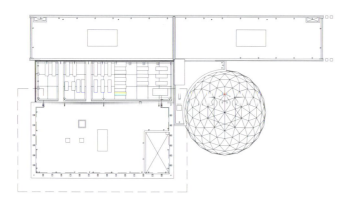

Roof floor plan

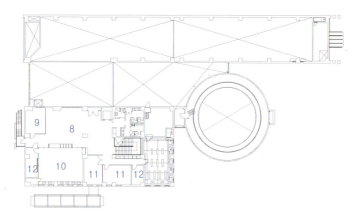

2nd floor plan

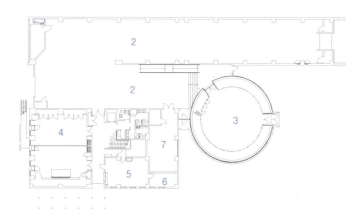

1st floor plan

▲ Open air auditorium

▲ Hall ▼ Exhibition hall

▲View of circular library from the road▼Building's exterior like clock tower

▲Outdoor swimming pool

▲Outdoor swimming pool with spectator facilities

▲Main view

이 센타는 원형의 도서관과 수직형의 스포츠 홀 및 관람시설을 갖춘 야외 수영장의 세 부분으로 구성되어 있다. 단순한 외관과 다양한 루트들과의 통합은 도시규모에 어울리는 랜드마크의 창조, 일관성의 제공 및 복지의 체계화를 위한 것이다. 밝은 격자 프레임, 날렵한 캐노피 그리고 시계탑과 같은 독립적인 요소는 구성하는 각 건물들을 연결하는 역할을 하며 보도(인도)에는 지각에 의한 자극을 유도한다. 디자인은 실용적이고 기품있게 설계되었으며 지역 주민들의 교육과 발전을 촉진시킬 수 있도록 고안되었다.

The Center integrates three component, a circular library, a rectilinear sports hall, and a set of outdoor swimming pools with spectator facilities. Simplified forms and multiple routes are integrated to organize the site, create civic landmarks and provide coherence at the urban scale. Independent elements, such as a bright grid frame, slender canopies, and a clock tower link the constituent buildings and offer perceptual stimuli at the pedestrian level. The design is practical and modest; the facility is conceived to foster the growth and education of the local community°Øs inhabitants.

▲Building with trass roof

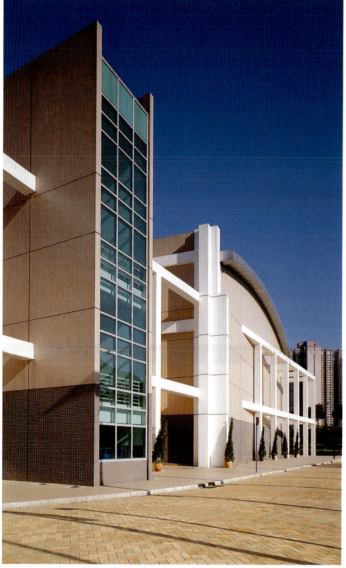

▲Building with bright grid frame

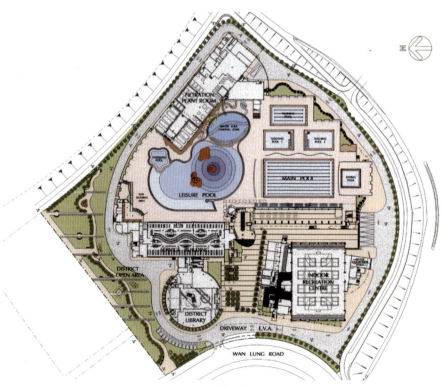

Site plan

대지위치 : 홍콩 Tseung Kwan O
대지면적 : 41,960㎡
연 면 적 : 12,750㎡
건축면적 : 11,420㎡
구　　조 : 철근콘크리트

Location : Tseung Kwan O, Hong Kong
Site area : 41,960㎡
Total floor area : 12,750㎡
Building area : 11,420㎡
Structure : Reinforced concrete

▲Brick – topped road

Mayfield Hotel

조경설계 : 정림개발
건축설계 : 엄이건축
시　공 : (주)대우건설, (주)오구종합건설
대지위치 : 서울특별시 강서구 외발산동 산 53-1
조경면적 :
대지면적 : 64,794.00㎡
건축면적 : 11,465.71㎡
연면적 : 31,638.27㎡
규　모 : 지하2층, 지상 6층
주차대수 : 536대
외부마감 : 신토석 치장쌓기, Base panel, 화강석버너마감,
　　　　　드라이비트, 동판지붕
사　진 : 이병일

Landscape design : Junglim Landscape Architects Inc.
Architecture design : AUM & LEE ARCHITECTS
　　　　　　　　　　ASSOCIATES
Construction : Daewoo Engineering Construction Co., Ltd,
　　　　　　　OGOO Construction Co.,Ltd
Landscaped area :
Site area : 64,794.00㎡
Building area : 11,465.71㎡
Total floor area : 31,638.27㎡
Stories : B2, 6FL
Parking capacity : 536 cars
Ext. finish : Finished cement laying, Base panel,
　　　　　　Granite flamed, Drivit, Copper roof,
Photographer : Lee byoung il

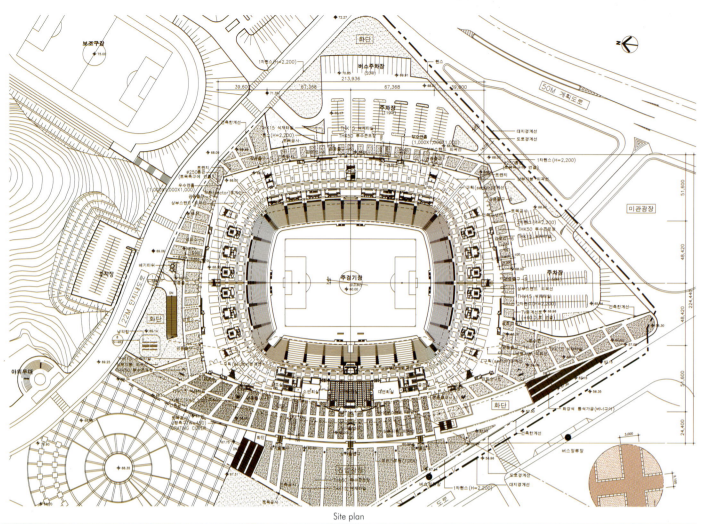

Site plan

Landscape plan

시　　공 : 삼성물산(주) 건설부문
조경설계 : (주)성호 엔지니어링
건축설계 : 삼우설계 + SCAV
대지위치 : 경기도 수원시 팔달구 우만동 228번지 일원
지역지구 : 자연녹지지역, 운동장시설지구
대지면적 : 425,000.00㎡
건축면적 : 30,937.02㎡
연 면 적 : 66,595.04㎡
조경면적 : 180,285.00㎡
규　　모 : 지상 4층, 지하 2층
구　　조 : 철근콘크리트조 + 철골조, PC 스탠드
수용인원 : 44,047 석
월드컵 시 가용주차대수 : 소형 3,334대, 대형 37대
주요외부마감 : 노출 콘크리트, 단층피막지붕재 + 폴리카보네이트쉬트

Construction : Samsung Corporation Engineering & Construction Group
Landscape architure design : Sngho Engineering
Architecture design : Samoo Architects & Engineers + SCAV
Site / District : Natural greenery area, Urban planning district
Site area : 425,000.00㎡
Building area : 30,937.02㎡
Total Floor area : 66,595.04㎡
Landscaped area : 180,285.00㎡
Building size : 4FL, 2B
Structure : Reinforced Concrete + Steel, PC Stand
Capacity : 44,047 Seats
Parking at the FIFA World Cup Games : 3,334 Cars, 37 Buses
Ext. finish : Exposed Concrete (Stadium)
　　　　　　 Single Membrane Roofing + Poly Carbonate Sheet (Roof)

▲Bird's eye view

▲View from North—east road

▲The square around stadium

수원시는 이미 국내 최고의 잔디구장을 보유하고 있으며, 풍부한 국제경기 경험을 축적하여 95, 96년에만 애틀랜타 올림픽 대표팀의 평가전 4회를 비롯해 국가대표팀 초청경기, 코리안 컵 대회 등 큰 경기를 성공적으로 개최하였다. 또한 수원을 연고지로 삼성 블루윙즈 축구단이 95년 12월 15일 국내 9번째 프로축구단으로 창단하였다. 김호 감독을 필두로 최강의 코칭 스태프와 선수진을 갖춘 삼성블루윙즈는 창단과 동시에 한국 축구계에 신선한 돌풍으로 부상하여 98 정규리그, 99 슈퍼티켓링크컵 등에서 우승하여 수원 및 경기도의 축구 붐 조성에 기여하였다. 그러한 기반으로 한국 프로축구 96 정규리그 개막전을 치르는 등 모든 경기를 성공적으로 개최한 수원은 매 경기마다 3만명 수용의 경기장이 연일 매진 기록했으며, 96~98 시즌 통산 평균 13,241명의 관중이 참여하여 전국 1위의 뜨거운 열기로, 홈팀은 물론 원정팀들도 수준 높은 경기를 펼치면서 한국 프로축구의 문화를 한 단계 끌어올리는데 기여하고 있다. 수원시는 이런 풍부한 경험을 바탕으로 세계인의 가슴속에 길이 남을 성공적인 월드컵 축구경기

를 개최하기 위해 1994년에 2002년 월드컵 유치를 신청하고 다방면으로 노력하여 1995년에는 16개 후보도시에 선정되었다. 이에 시는 유치위원회를 발족하고, FIFA가 정한 필수조건을 충족하고도 남는 국내 초유의 축구전용구장을 건립하기 위하여 총력을 다하고, 시민 결의대회 및 단결통장 갖기 등을 통해 시민의 뜻이 인정되어, 1997년에 드디어 월드컵개최도시로 확정되었고, 수원 축구 전용 경기장은 명실공히 역사적인 월드컵 유치구장으로 남게 되었다. 계획적인 특징이나 의의를 찾는다면 첫째, 진정한 한국축구의 메카를 조성하기 위하여 마스터플랜 수립 시부터 참여한 건축주의 의지를 살려, 보조구장 외에 잔디연습구장 2면을 설치하고, 지역주민들이 사용할 수 있는 클레이 구장도 설치한 것이다. 국내에 이렇게 한 부지 내에 5면의 축구경기장이 설치된 곳은 유래가 없다. 아쉬운 점은 처음 계획대로 지하에 스포렉스와 기타 부대시설이 구성되지 못한 것이지만, 그것은 누구의 잘못이라 할 수는 없는 것이다. 둘째, 경기장이라는 본질적인 기능을 생각할 때 효율과 기능적인 면이 형태나 디자인을 지배하게 되어

마땅히 특별한 이미지를 줄 수 있는 것은 지붕 뿐이라 할 수 있다. 함께 설계를 한 프랑스의 SCAU와 협의하여 가장 한국적인 건축의 특징 또한 지붕이라고 결론을 내렸다. 전체적인 건물 비례에서 지붕이 큰 편인 동양의 목구조의 공포와 처마를 이미지화하기로 하여 지금의 지붕이 계획되었다. 처음부터 필요없이 길다느니, 날개 같다느니 하는 의견이 분분하였지만 이는 한국 전통건축의 지붕구조를 은유화의 결과인 것이다. 초기엔 남·북측 스탠드에도 지붕이 계획되어 전체 스탠드에 지붕이 있었으나, 공사비 절감차원에서 이 또한 조정되었다.

셋째, 간결하고 명쾌한 구조, 그리고 오랫동안 실증나지 않는 건축을 위해 구조미가 뛰어 나면서도 효율적인 구조가 채택되었다. 지붕의 보이는 부분은 단순 캔틸레버의 파이프 트러스를 봉강으로 바닥구조에 연결하여, 중력과 풍력에 모두 안전하게 하였다. 경제성, 안전성, 유지관리 등을 기본적으로 고려하여 스탠드 등 하부구조는 별개로 구분하여 PC와 노출 철근콘크리트로 처리하였다.

넷째, 많은 사람이 모이는 이런 대형공간에서는 안

• 벽돌 선택은 실제 쌓아놓은 것을 보아야 합니다. • 바닥벽돌의 선택은 실제 깔아놓은 것을 보아야 합니다.

벽돌건축에 관한 모든 정보가 한자리에

건축자재정보 교환의 장
건축인 모임의 장
대도벽돌 전시관

최고의 기술과 최신시설,
大 都 의 장인정신이 빚어낸 각종 점토벽돌과
헬시 다기능 바닥재, 연결보강재등 벽돌 관련 제품의
모든 것을 직접 체험하고 확인하실 수 있습니다.

대도벽돌은 37년을 한결같이 우수한 품질의 점토벽돌과 헬시 다기능 보·차도용 바닥벽돌, 연결보강재 등을 생산해온 건축자재전문 생산산업체입니다. 국내관련업체들중 최초로 KS 마크 획득과 ISO 9001 품질인증 및 국제공인기관에 의한 ISO 14001 인증, 건설교통부로 부터 벽돌벽 조적공법으로 신기술 제198호를 지정받은 대도벽돌은 충남예산과 충북괴산에 국내 최대의 선진 자동화 생산설비를 갖추고 끊임없는 기술개발과 고품질의 제품생산으로 소비자의 요구에 부응하고자 노력하고 있습니다.
대도벽돌은 또한 보유하고 있는 기술 인력을 통하여 벽돌건축에 대한 설계 및 시공상의 기술 지원은 물론 벽돌생산에서 판매, 시공, 하자보수에 이르는 벽돌건축의 모든 부분에 대한 도움을 드리고 있습니다.

❖ 신동방사옥

❖ 신도리코 성수동 공장

❖ SK타운 하우스

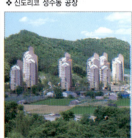
❖ 용인 보정리 아파트

❖ 헬시 다기능 바닥벽돌 시공사례 ("걷고 싶은 거리" 강남 압구정동)

신개념 바닥벽돌
보·차도 겸용의 고강도 바닥벽돌
헬시 다기능 바닥벽돌

• **모서리가 깨지지 않습니다!**
이제 까지의 사각바닥벽돌은 모서리 깨짐 현상이 심했으나 모서리를 45°접은 대도벽돌의 "헬시 다기능 바닥벽돌"은 모서리가 깨지지 않습니다.

• **단단합니다!**
선별된 원료와 높은 화도로 구워 40톤의 차량무게를 견딜 만큼 높은 강도를 가지고 있습니다.

• **생태계를 보존 합니다!**
시멘트가 아닌 점토소재로서 우수가 지하로 스며 들어 지하 생태계를 보존 합니다.

벽돌사면(모서리)45° 처리
200mm
99mm
57mm
돌기부위

· 바닥점토벽돌 의장등록/등록 제30-0310714호
· 다기능 바닥점토벽돌 실용신안등록/등록 제0314074호

한남대교 올림픽로 동호대교
미성APT 현대백화점
고속터미널 살림 삼화호텔 압구정역
(구)상아탑학원
경부고속도로 남서울웨딩홀 대도벽돌 전시관
신사역 안세병원
강남대로
❖ 위치도

❖ 대도벽돌 전시관 내부

 대도벽돌
서울시 강남구 신사동 527번지 대도벽돌전시관 대표전화:(02)543-0092 FAX:(02)549-8198
전시관:(02)548-4428 http://www.brick.co.kr e-mail:brick@brick.co.kr 소비자고충처리센타: 080-543-0090

울산 동천체육관

인천문학경기장

SK 반포주유소

Mak/lax

Use Your
Imagination
Use Our
Technology
...Makmax

**세계를 변하게 한
테크놀러지 드디어 한국에**

세계 건축분야의 역사를 계속
바꾸게 한 막구조 기술이 드디어
한국에 그 분야를 확대해 가고
있습니다.

막이 갖고 있는 독자적인 표현성
이나 특성이 만들어내는 예술적인
조형미는 압도적이라고 할 수
있는 존재감을 자랑하고 다른
소재의 추종을 불허합니다.

각 나라의 문화와 풍토에 어울
리는 높은 설계기술과 오랜
세월에 걸친 시공실적을 살려
한국 건축에 가일층의 비약을
서포트하기 위해 Taiyo Kogyo
그룹은 본격적으로 시동합니다.

세계 No.1 膜 구조메이커

Mak/lax   한국타이요코교주식회사

135-934 서울특별시 강남구 역삼동 824-19 동경빌딩 7층
Tel. 02-561-6814 Fax. 02-561-0900
http:www.taiyokogyo.net/kr

TAIYO KOGYO GROUP   BIRDAIR   Shade Structures BIRDAIR

(일본)	Taiyo Kogyo Corporation
(미국)	Birdair, inc.
(오스트레일리아)	Shade Structures Birdair (SSB)
(독일)	Birdair Europe Stromeyer GmbH
(중국)	Shanghai Taiyo Kogyo Co., Ltd.
(타이완)	Taiwan Taiyo Kogyo Inc.(TTI)
(태국)	Taiyo Kogyo (Thailand) Co.,Ltd.

Beijing, Shingapore, Maleysia

KL 모노레일 스테이션

동경임해공원